KNITTING
Wildlife

To the memory of Dian Fossey, who dedicated her life
to the research and conservation of the
Mountain Gorillas of Rwanda.

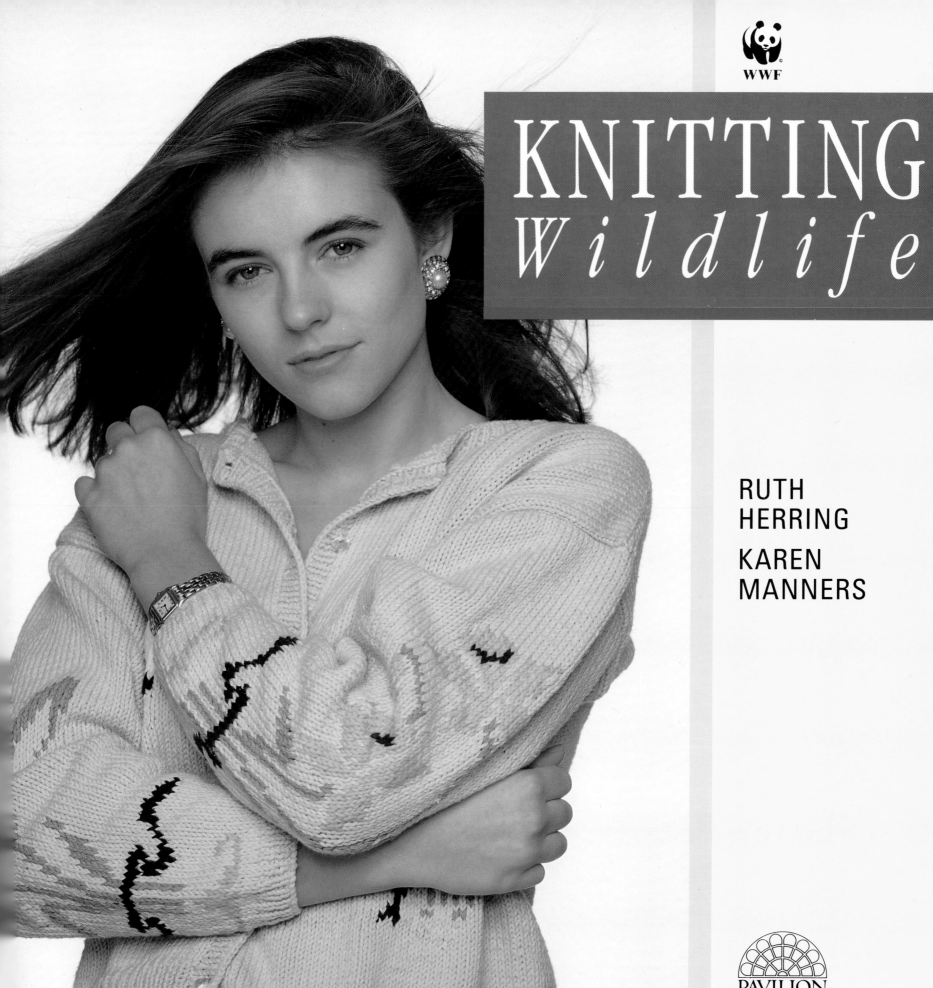

WWF

KNITTING
Wildlife

**RUTH
HERRING**

**KAREN
MANNERS**

PAVILION
MICHAEL JOSEPH

First published in Great Britain in 1989 by
PAVILION BOOKS LIMITED
196 Shaftesbury Avenue, London WC2H 8JL
in association with Michael Joseph Limited
27 Wrights Lane, Kensington, W8 5TZ

Text and designs Copyright © Ruth Herring and
Karen Manners 1989
Photographs Copyright © Pavilion Books Limited 1989

Designed by Janet James
Photography by Kim Knott

LIBRARY OF CONGRESS NUMBER 89-61380

ISBN 1 85145 525 6

Printed and bound in Spain
by Graficas Estella

WWF World Wide Fund for Nature
WWF continues to be known as World Wildlife Fund in
Australia, Canada and the USA.

CONTENTS

Badgers have suffered at the hands of man for centuries. They have been shot, trapped, poisoned and hunted with dogs. All this in the name of sport, for their pelts and tails which are used to make shaving-brushes, or as alleged crop-raiders, poultry-thieves, or carriers of disease. Their habitat has decreased as woodlands have been cleared and hedgerows ripped up and they constantly run the risk of being killed on roads and electrified railway lines. Unsur-prisingly, they have become rare in several parts of their range, which stretches from Western Europe across most of temperate Asia to Japan. On the whole, however, Badgers are sturdy and adaptable and they are still quite common in areas where they are not excessively persecuted and habitat destruction has not been too great. In such places they can become quite tame and can be a delight to watch playing and feeding in woods and fields.

BADGERS
and Wildflowers

► A timid Badger is seen here peeping through the lush undergrowth of meadow flowers. Bulky yarn is used to create a luxurious and richly colored box sweater. Worked in two pieces, the stripy bands and collar are added later.

SIZE
One size to fit 32–38in chest.

MATERIALS
Pingouin Chunky
4 × 1¾oz balls Noir (shade 16)
3 × 1¾oz balls Persan (shade 07)
2 × 1¾oz balls each of Blanc (shade 01), Feu (05)
1 × 1¾oz ball each of Bleu Nuit (shade 09), Rose Indien (06)
Pingouin Mohican, flecked bulky
3 × 1¾oz balls Souris (shade 11)
Pingouin France + (used double)
3 × 1¾oz balls Violet (shade 26)
2 × 1¾oz balls Soleil (shade 10)
A pair each of sizes 8 and 10 knitting needles
Stitch holder

GAUGE
13 sts. and 16 rows to 4in over pat. worked on size 10 needles

To save time, take time to check gauge.

NOTES
When working motif, use separate, small balls of yarn. When joining in a new color, leave an end of about 2in for weaving in later. When changing color, twist yarns together at back of work to avoid making a hole. If preferred, small areas such as flower centers and green stalks may be worked in duplicate stitch, see "Know-How" section at back of book.

RIGHT SIDE
** Using size 8 needles and noir, cast on 31 sts.
Rib row 1: K.1 violet, * p.1 noir, k.1 violet; rep from * to end.
Rib row 2: P.1 violet, * k.1 noir, p.1 violet; rep. from * to end.
Rep. these 2 rows 3 times more, then rib row 1 once more.
Inc. row: Using noir, rib 1, m.1, * rib 3, m.1; rep. from * to end: 42 sts.
Change to size 10 needles and work from row 1 of chart, shaping sleeves by inc. 1 st. each end of 5th and every foll. 4th row until there are 68 sts., then inc. 1 st. each end of next 2 rows: 72 sts.
Next row: Cast on 5 sts., then k. in pat. across these sts. and to end of row, turn.

"Badgers and Wildflowers" modeled by singer Kim Wilde. Her sixth LP, Close, has attained Gold Record Status in ten countries. 1989 began with her sixteenth UK top forty hit. Kim devotes much time to environmental issues.

BADGERS AND WILDFLOWERS

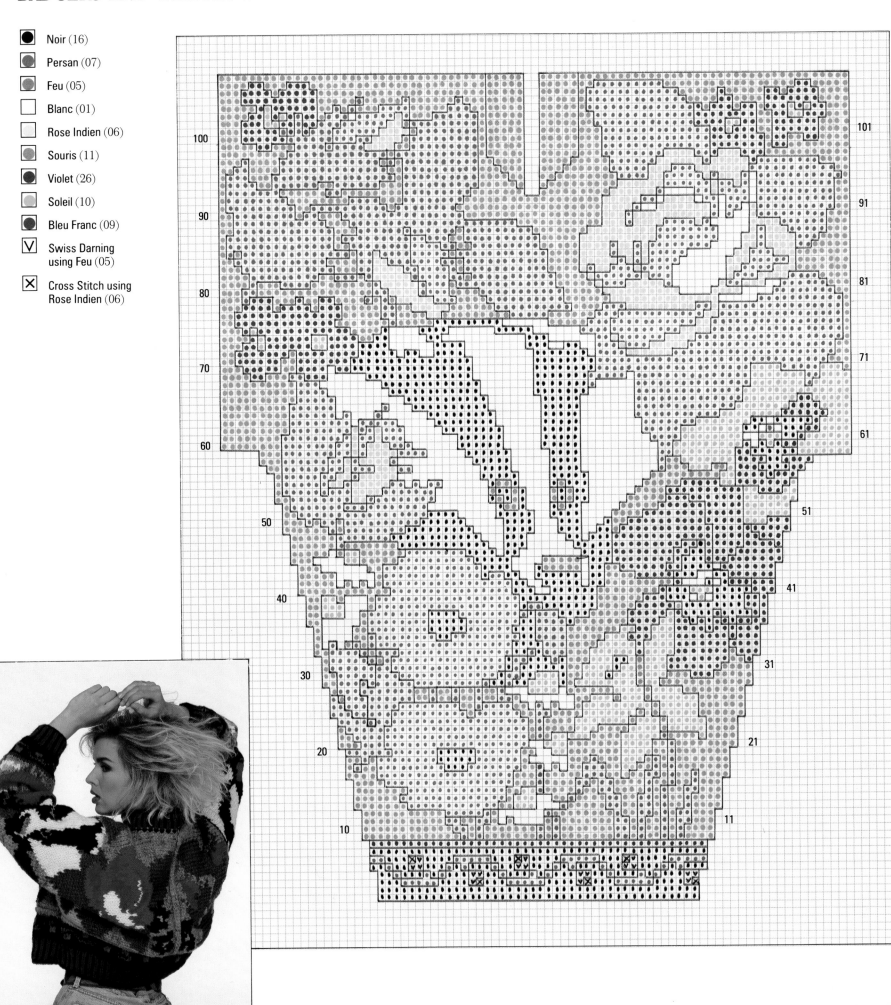

Legend:

- ● Noir (16)
- ● Persan (07)
- ● Feu (05)
- □ Blanc (01)
- □ Rose Indien (06)
- ● Souris (11)
- ● Violet (26)
- □ Soleil (10)
- ● Bleu Franc (09)
- V Swiss Darning using Feu (05)
- X Cross Stitch using Rose Indien (06)

Next row: Cast on 5 sts., then p. in pat. across these sts. and to end of row: 82 sts.

Cont. working even until row 92 has been completed.

Next row: K.40 sts. in pat., bind off 2 sts., k. to end. **

Back yoke

Keeping work even, cont. working in pat. on first 40 sts. only until row 108 has been completed from chart.

Bind off. Return to rem. 40 sts.

Shape front neck

With WS facing, rejoin yarn and p.2 tog., p. to end in pat. Cont. working from chart, dec. 1 st. at neck edge only on every row until 35 sts. rem. Then work even until row 108 from chart has been completed.

Bind off.

LEFT SIDE

Work as given for right side from ** to **.

Shape front neck

Cont. working on first 40 sts. only, dec. 1 st. at neck edge only on next and every foll. row until 35 sts. rem. Then work even until row 108 from chart has been completed. Bind off.

Return to rem. 40 sts.

Back yoke

With WS facing, rejoin yarn to first st. and p. to end. Work even until row 108 has been completed from chart. Bind off.

COLLAR

With WS tog., backstitch center front seam.

Using size 8 needles and souris, with RS facing, pick up and k.36 sts. around left side of neck, 1 st. at center front seam, then pick up and k.36 sts. around right side of neck: 73 sts.

P.1 row.

Rib row 1: K.1 noir, *p.1 souris, k.1 noir; rep. from * to end.

Rib row 2: P.1 violet, *k.1 noir, p.1 violet; rep. from * to end.

Rib row 3: K.1 violet, * p.1 noir, k.1 violet; rep. from * to end.

Rep. rib rows 2 and 3 twice more.

Using noir, rib 1 row.

Bind off in rib.

Join collar seam, then with WS tog., backstitch center back seam.

FRONT EDGE

Using souris and size 10 needles, with RS of lower front edge facing, pick up and k.39 sts. to center front, 1 st. at center front seam, then 39 sts. to left side: 79 sts.

Bind off purlwise.

Rep. the same for back edge.

BACK AND FRONT BANDS (Make 2)

Using size 8 needles and noir, cast on 71 sts.

Rep. 2 rib rows as given for right side for 9 rows.

Inc. row: Using noir, * rib 8, m.1; rep. from * to last 7 sts, rib 7: 79 sts.

Change to size 10 needles and work 2 rows noir, then work rows 3–8 from chart, placing jacquard pat. as follows:

Row 3: K.9 noir, * k.5 persan, k.9 noir; rep. from * to end. When row 8 has been completed, using souris, k.1 row. Bind off purlwise.

TO FINISH

Block and press pieces lightly under a damp cloth, foll yarn label instructions. With WS tog., backstitch front and back bands to bound-off edges at lower edge of yoke. Join side and sleeve seams. Embroider cross stitch details on cuffs and lower edges as shown on chart.

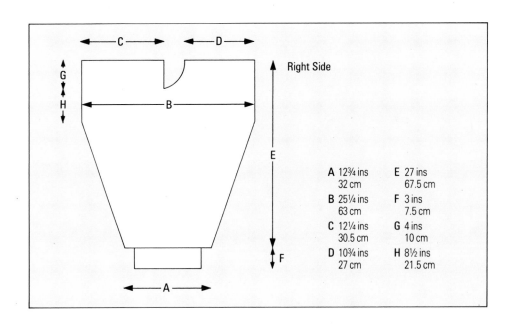

A 12¾ ins 32 cm	E 27 ins 67.5 cm
B 25¼ ins 63 cm	F 3 ins 7.5 cm
C 12¼ ins 30.5 cm	G 4 ins 10 cm
D 10¾ ins 27 cm	H 8½ ins 21.5 cm

The Tiger is the largest of all the cats, and now sadly also one of the rarest. It leads a largely solitary life in the jungles and forests of Asia, hunting down game such as wild pigs and deer. Where these have become scarce, Tigers will turn for food to domestic livestock and, very rarely, man himself. For this reason, and also for their bones, which are used in traditional medicines, and their valuable skin, they have been relentlessly hunted almost everywhere. Several popu-lations are now extinct while others, such as the Javan and Siberian Tigers, are critically endangered. In total perhaps 3,000 Tigers now survive in the wild, most of these in the Indian subcontinent in India, Bangladesh, Nepal, and Burma. In India the "Operation Tiger" conservation cam-paign has succeeded in halting the decline, at least tempo-rarily, although the ever-increasing human population makes the Tiger's future even there look far from certain.

White and Indian
TIGERS

▶ Dignified and proud, the creature almost comes alive with the use of color and attention to detail. Choose from the rich golds of the Indian Tiger or the pale hues of the rare White Tiger. The classic sweater or elegant ladies' suit may be knitted in either colorway.

SIZES
Sweater
To fit 32/34 (36, 38, 40, 42)in chest.

Skirt
To fit 34 (36, 38)in hips.

MATERIALS
Sweater (Men's or Ladies')
Emu Superwash medium-weight 100% wool
9 (10, 10, 11, 11) × 1¾oz. balls MC (shade 3019 or 3006)
3 × 1¾oz balls First CC (shade 3070 or 3009)
1 × 1¾oz ball each of:
2nd CC (shade 3078)
3rd CC (shade 3012 or 3016)
4th CC (shade 3006 or 3079)

Skirt
3 × 1¾oz balls MC (shade 3019 or 3006)
1 × 1¾oz ball each of:
First CC (shade 3070 or 3009)
2nd CC (shade 3012 or 3016)
3rd CC (shade 3006 or 3079)
A pair each of sizes 3 and 6 knitting needles

6in zipper to match skirt
Stitch holder

GAUGE
22 sts. and 30 rows to 4in over pat. worked on size 6 needles

To save time, take time to check gauge.

NOTES
Directions for larger sizes are given in parentheses ().
When working motifs, use separate, small balls of yarn.
When joining in a new color, leave an end of about 2in for weaving in later. When changing color, twist yarns together to avoid making a hole.

"White Tiger" modeled by Imran Khan, captain of Pakistan's Cricket team and one of cricket''s great all-rounders, hence the title of his autobiography, All-rounder, which was published last year.

Men's Sweater

BACK

** Using size 3 needles and MC, cast on 107 (113, 117, 123, 129) sts.

Rib row 1: K.1 , * p.1, k.1; rep. from * to end.

Rib row 2: P.1 , * k.1, p.1; rep. from * to end.

Rep. 2 rib rows for 3in, ending rib row 1.

Inc. row: Rib 6 (8, 10, 14, 16), m.1, * rib 12, m.1; rep. from * to last 5 (9, 11, 13, 17) sts., rib to end: 116 (122, 126, 132, 138) sts. **

*** Change to size 6 needles and work from row 17 (13, 9, 5, 1) of Chart A until row 162 (166, 170, 174, 176) has been completed.

Shape back neck

Next row: K.48 (51, 52, 53, 56) sts. in pat., turn and leave rem. sts. on a stitch holder. Work on these sts. only.

Keeping pat. correct, bind off 6 sts. at beg. of next and foll. alt. row. Bind off rem. 36 (39, 40, 41, 44) sts.

With RS facing, slip first 20 (20, 22, 26, 26) sts. onto a stitch holder.

Rejoin yarn to first stitch and k. in pat. to end.

Complete 2nd side of back neck to match first side, reversing all shaping. ***

FRONT

Work as given for back from ** to **.

**** Change to size 6 needles and work from row 17 (13, 9, 5, 1) of Chart B, until row 144 (148, 152, 156, 158) has been completed.

Shape front neck

Next row: K.48 (51, 53, 56, 59) sts., turn and leave rem. sts. on a stitch holder.

Work on these sts. only.

Dec. 1 st. at neck edge only on every row until 36 (39, 40, 41, 44) sts. rem., then work 9 (9, 8, 6, 6) rows even.

Bind off.

With RS facing, slip first 20 sts. onto a stitch holder.

Rejoin yarn to first st. and k. to end.

Complete 2nd side of front neck to match first side, reversing all shaping. ****

White

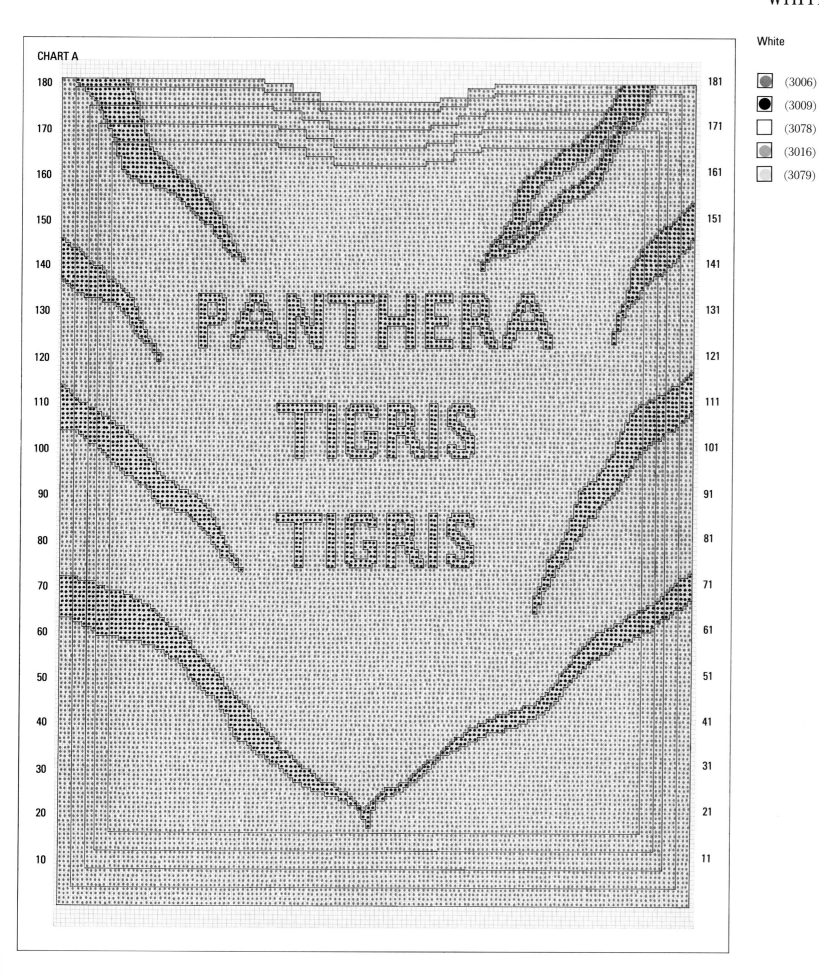

CHART A

- (3006)
- (3009)
- (3078)
- (3016)
- (3079)

INDIAN TIGER

Ladies' Sweater

BACK

** Using size 3 needles and MC, cast on 116 (122, 126, 132, 138) sts.

Work 7 rows st.st., ending with a k. row.

Next row (WS): Knit. **

Now work from *** to *** as given for men's back.

FRONT

Work from ** to ** as given for ladies' back, then from ****
to **** as given for men's front.

SLEEVES (Both versions)

Using size 3 needles and MC, cast on 51 (53, 55, 57, 57)
sts.

Work 2½in rib as given for men's back, ending rib row 1.

Inc. row: Rib 6 (6, 2, 4, 4), m.1, * rib 5, m.1; rep. from * to
last 5 (7, 3, 3, 3) sts., rib to end: 60 (62, 66, 68, 68) sts.

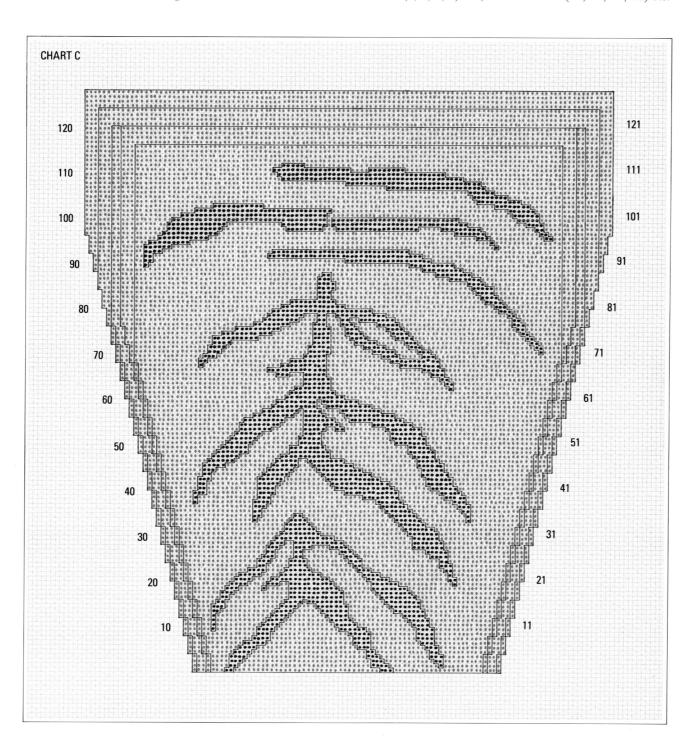

CHART C

Indian

● (3019)
● (3070)
□ (3078)
● (3012)
▨ (3006)

Change to size 6 needles and work from row 1 of Chart C, shaping sleeves as indicated on chart: 94 (100, 104, 110, 116) sts. When row 116 (120, 120, 124, 128) has been completed, bind off.

COLLAR (Both versions)
Join left shoulder seam.
Using size 3 needles and MC, with RS facing, pick up and k.15 sts. down right back neck, k.20 (20, 22, 26, 26) sts. from holder, pick up and k.16 sts. up left back neck, 21 (21, 23, 24, 24) sts. down left front neck, k.20 sts. from holder, pick up and k.21 (21, 23, 24, 24) sts. up right front neck: 113 (113, 119, 125, 125) sts.
P.1 row.
Rib row 1: K.2 CC, * p.1 MC, k.2 CC; rep. from * to end.
Rib row 2: P.2 CC, * k.1 MC, p.2 CC; rep. from * to end.
Rep. 2 rib rows for 9 rows for crewneck or 17 rows for high neck, then using CC, rib 1 row. Bind off in rib.

TO FINISH
Block and press pieces lightly under a damp cloth foll. yarn label instructions. Join right shoulder and collar seams. Sew in sleeves, then join side and sleeve seams. For ladies' sweater, press hem to inside along foldline and slipstitch in place.

"Indian Tiger" modeled by 1976 "Model of the Year", Marie Helvin, who has worked with Yves St Laurent, Helmut Newton and, of course, David Bailey, with whom she was married in 1975. She is the subject of his acclaimed book Trouble and Strife *and is author of her own book,* Catwalk.

Skirt

Using size 3 needles and MC, cast on 76 (82, 88) sts.
Work 7 rows st.st., ending with a k. row.
Next row (WS): Knit.
Change to size 6 needles and work from row 1 of Chart D for skirt back and Chart E for skirt front, dec. 1 st. at beg. of row 120: 67 (73, 79) sts.

Change to size 3 needles and using MC, work 3½in in k.1, p.1 rib.
Bind off in rib.

TO FINISH

Block and press pieces lightly under a damp cloth foll. yarn label instructions. Join side seams leaving 6in on left side for zipper. Sew in zipper. Finish hem as for sweater.

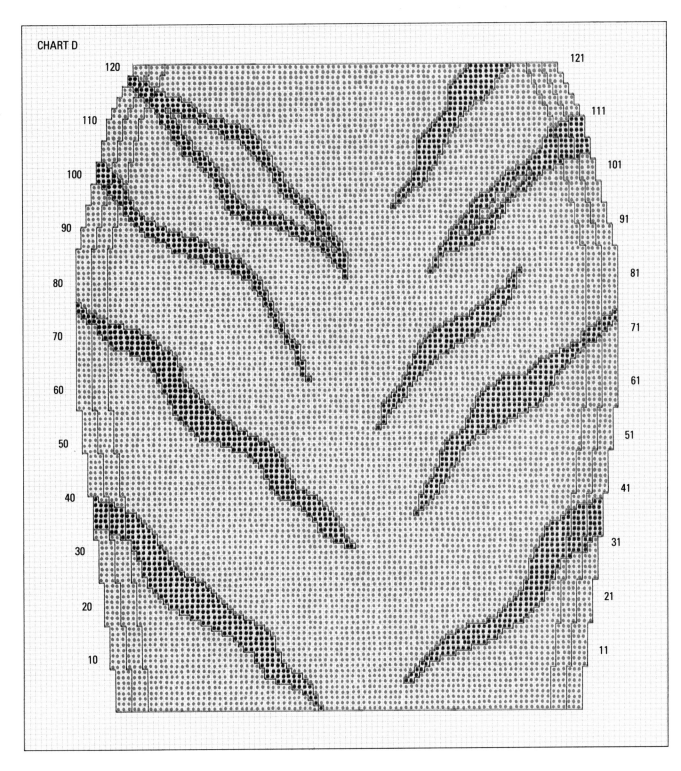

CHART D

17

INDIAN TIGER

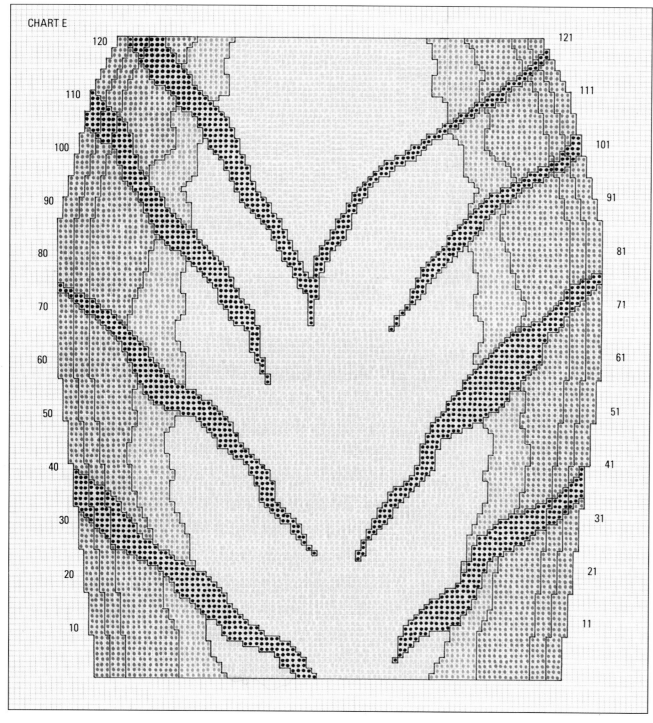

CHART E

120   121
110   111
100   101
90   91
80   81
70   71
60   61
50   51
40   41
30   31
20   21
10   11

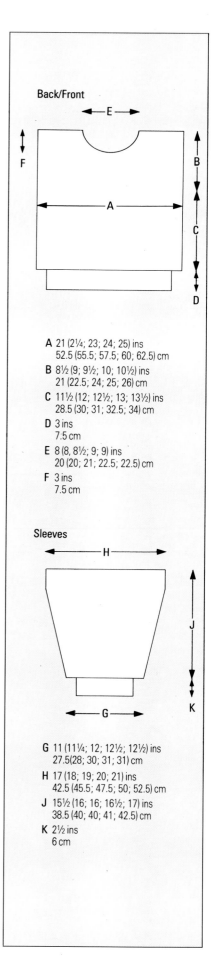

Back/Front

E

F   B

A

C

D

A 21 (2¼; 23; 24; 25) ins
  52.5 (55.5; 57.5; 60; 62.5) cm

B 8½ (9; 9½; 10; 10½) ins
  21 (22.5; 24; 25; 26) cm

C 11½ (12; 12½; 13; 13½) ins
  28.5 (30; 31; 32.5; 34) cm

D 3 ins
  7.5 cm

E 8 (8, 8½; 9; 9) ins
  20 (20; 21; 22.5; 22.5) cm

F 3 ins
  7.5 cm

Sleeves

H

J

G   K

G 11 (11¼; 12; 12½; 12½) ins
  27.5(28; 30; 31; 31) cm

H 17 (18; 19; 20; 21) ins
  42.5 (45.5; 47.5; 50; 52.5) cm

J 15½ (16; 16; 16½; 17) ins
  38.5 (40; 40; 41; 42.5) cm

K 2½ ins
  6 cm

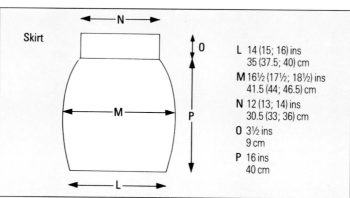

Skirt

N

O

M   P

L

L 14 (15; 16) ins
  35 (37.5; 40) cm

M 16½ (17½; 18½) ins
  41.5 (44; 46.5) cm

N 12 (13; 14) ins
  30.5 (33; 36) cm

O 3½ ins
  9 cm

P 16 ins
  40 cm

Despite their enormous strength and imposing appearance, Gorillas, mankind's closest living relatives, are generally harmless and peaceable creatures. Three distinct populations live in different parts of the great central African rainforests. The Western Lowland Gorilla inhabits forests in Cameroon, Gabon, and adjacent countries and numbers perhaps 40,000 in total, but the two others are much rarer. These are the Eastern Lowland Gorilla of eastern Zaire, and the Mountain Gorilla, which lives in the Virunga volcano's region of eastern Zaire, Rwanda and Uganda, and in the Bwindi Forest Reserve in Uganda. The Mountain Gorilla in particular is severely endangered as fewer than 500 now survive. Gorillas everywhere are threatened by the clearing of forests for timber and conversion of land to agriculture, or even, in the case of the Mountain Gorillas, to obtain skulls and hands to sell to tourists.

Mountain
GORILLA
of Rwanda

SIZES
To fit 27 (30, 32, 33)in chest.
Age 7 (9, 11, 13) years.

MATERIALS
Hayfield Grampian Chunky
1 × 1¾oz ball each of Black (shade 036024) and Tarn Blue (shade 036063)
Hayfield Lugarno (mohair)
4 × 1¾oz balls Matterhorn (shade 094059)
1 × 1¾oz ball each of St. Moritz (shade 093004) and Champery (093012)
A pair each of sizes 8 and 10 knitting needles
Stitch holder

GAUGE
14 sts. and 18 rows to 4in over pat. worked on size 10 needles

To save time, take time to check gauge.

NOTES
Directions for larger sizes are given in parentheses ().
When working motif, use separate, small balls of yarn.

When joining in a new color, leave an end of about 2in for weaving in later. When changing color, twist yarns together at back of work to avoid making a hole.

BACK
** Using size 8 needles and matterhorn, cast on 55, (59, 65, 69) sts.
Rib row 1: K.1 St. Moritz, * p.1 matterhorn, k.1 St. Moritz; rep. from * to end.
Rib row 2: P.1 St. Moritz, * k.1 matterhorn, p.1 St. Moritz; rep. from * to end.
Rep these 2 rib rows for 2in, ending rib row 1.
Next row: Using matterhorn, p.1, m.1, rib to end: 56 (60, 66, 70) sts. **
Change to size 10 needles and using matterhorn, work 62 (66, 76, 82) rows st.st.
Bind off 17 (19, 21, 22) sts., k.21 (21, 23, 25), bind off 17 (19, 21, 22).
Leave center 22 (22, 24, 26) sts. on a stitch holder.

FRONT
Work as given for back from ** to **.
Change to size 10 needles and work from row 15 (11, 5, 1) of chart until row 62 (62, 64, 66) has been completed.

Quick and simple to knit, this soft mohair and bulky-knit child's sweater will be a favorite! The back and sleeves are hairy like a Gorilla's, and the face is in realistic detail.

MOUNTAIN GORILLA

Shape front neck

Next row: Keeping pat. correct, k.23 (25, 28, 30), turn and leave rem. sts. on a stitch holder.

Work on these sts. only. Dec. 1 st. at neck edge only on every row until 17 (19, 21 22) sts. rem.

Work 7 (7, 8, 7) rows even. Bind off.

Return to sts. on stitch holder.

With RS facing, slip first 10 sts. onto a stitch holder, rejoin yarn to first st. and k. in pat. to end.

Complete 2nd side of front neck to match first side, reversing all shaping.

SLEEVES (Both alike)

Using size 8 needles and matterhorn, cast on 27 (29, 31, 33) sts.

Work in rib as given for back for 2in, ending rib row 2.

Inc. row: Using matterhorn, rib 2 (4, 6, 8), * m.1, rib 5; rep. from * to end: 32 (34, 36, 38) sts.

Change to size 10 needles and using matterhorn, work in st.st., inc. 1 st. each end of 5th and every foll. 4th row until there are 50 (54, 58, 62) sts.

Work even until sleeve measures 12¼ (13, 14½, 16¼)in from beg. Bind off.

NECKBAND

Join left shoulder seam.

Using size 8 needles and matterhorn, with RS facing, k. across 22 (22, 24, 26) sts. from stitch holder, pick up and k.15 (15, 17, 17) sts. down left front neck, k. across 10 sts. from stitch holder, pick up and k. 14 (14, 16, 16) sts. up right front neck: 61 (61, 67, 69) sts.

P.1 row.

Starting rib row 1, rep. 2 rib rows as given for back for 9 rows. Then using matterhorn, work 1 row rib.

Bind off in rib.

TO FINISH

Block and press pieces lightly under a damp cloth, foll. yarn label instructions. Join right shoulder and collar seam. Sew in sleeves. Join side and sleeve seams.

"Gorillas" modeled by
Lydia Raghavan, playmate
of Rory Robertson, who
models the Panda Jacket.

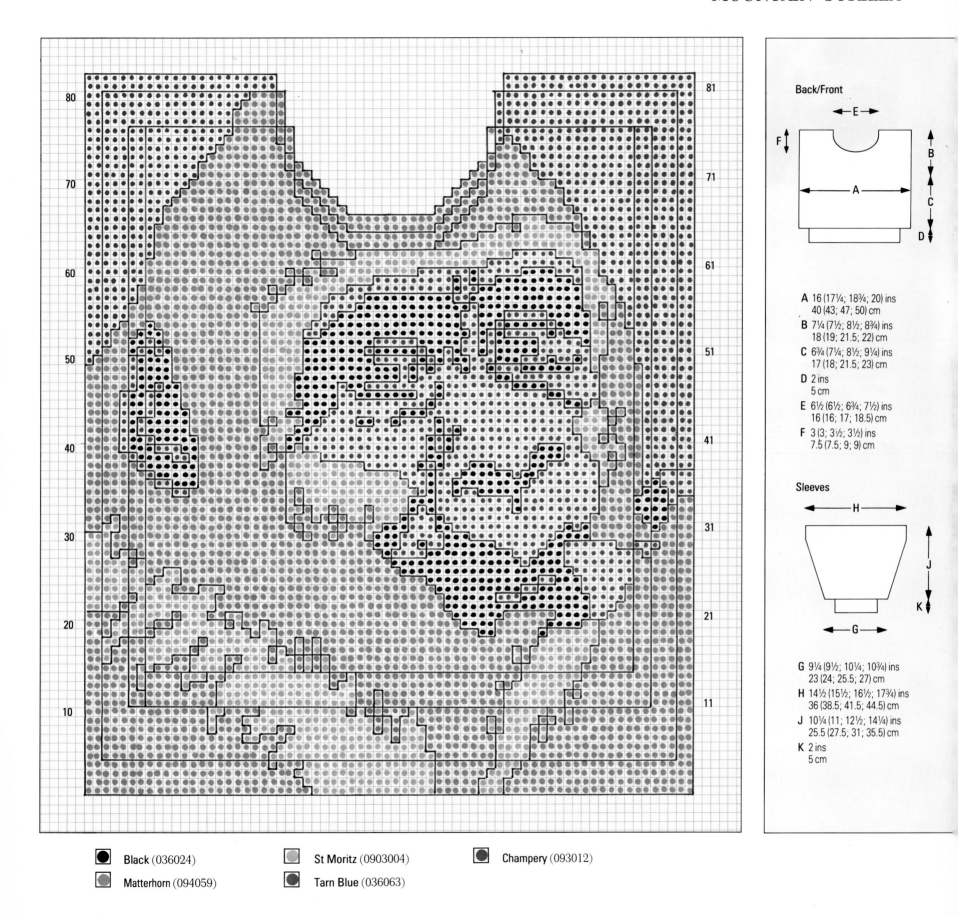

Back/Front

A 16 (17¼; 18¾; 20) ins
40 (43; 47; 50) cm

B 7¼ (7½; 8½; 8¾) ins
18 (19; 21.5; 22) cm

C 6¾ (7¼; 8½; 9¼) ins
17 (18; 21.5; 23) cm

D 2 ins
5 cm

E 6½ (6½; 6¾; 7½) ins
16 (16; 17; 18.5) cm

F 3 (3; 3½; 3½) ins
7.5 (7.5; 9; 9) cm

Sleeves

G 9¼ (9½; 10¼; 10¾) ins
23 (24; 25.5; 27) cm

H 14½ (15½; 16½; 17¾) ins
36 (38.5; 41.5; 44.5) cm

J 10¼ (11; 12½; 14¼) ins
25.5 (27.5; 31; 35.5) cm

K 2 ins
5 cm

● Black (036024)   ● St Moritz (0903004)   ● Champery (093012)

● Matterhorn (094059)   ● Tarn Blue (036063)

The Giant Panda, since 1961 the symbol of WWF, is perhaps the best known and best loved of all rare animals. Fewer than 1,300 of them survive in the remote forested hills of south-west China where they are under constant threat from loss of habitat by logging and the spread of agriculture, accidental capture in wild-animal snares, and periodic mass dying-off of the bamboo plants on which they feed. Fortunately, over half of all wild Pandas are protected in twelve reserves set up specially for them. Since 1978 scientists have been studying Pandas in one of the most important of these, Woolong Reserve in Sichuan Province, in the hope that a better understanding of their habits may make it easier to ensure their survival. Plans for the future include the setting up of more reserves, planting of bamboo to provide more feeding areas for Pandas, and reintroducing them into suitable areas where they used to occur.

Giant PANDA

▶ Sporty designs influence the Giant Panda garments. The adult's sweater features a football-style motif on the back, while the child's, a traditional baseball jacket motif. The Chinese characters mean "More Effort Needed To Save The Panda." The bright colors and bold Panda add to the sporty feel.

SIZES
To fit 34 (36, 38, 40)in chest

MATERIALS
Pingouin Chunky
15 × 1¾oz balls Feu (shade 05)
5 (5, 5, 6) × 1¾oz balls Blanc (shade 01)
2 × 1¾oz balls Noir (shade 16)
1 × 1¾oz ball Persan (shade 07)
A pair each of sizes 8 and 10 knitting needles
Stitch holder

GAUGE
13 sts. and 18 rows to 4in over motif on size 10 needles

To save time, take time to check gauge.

NOTES
Directions for larger sizes shown in parentheses ().
When working motif, use separate, small balls of yarn.
When joining in a new color, leave an end of about 2in for weaving in later and when changing color, twist yarns together at back of work to avoid making a hole.

BACK
** Using size 8 needles and noir, cast on 57 (59, 63, 67) sts.
Working in k.1, p.1 rib, work 1 row noir, 11 rows blanc, then 1 row noir.
Inc. row: Using noir, rib 1 (2, 4, 6), m.1, *rib 7, m.1; rep from * to last 0 (1, 3, 5) sts., rib to end: 66 (68, 72, 76) sts. **
Change to size 10 needles and using feu, work 32 (36, 44, 48) rows st.st.
Now work from Chart B, placing row 1 of chart after first 16 (17, 19, 21) sts. feu.
When row 10 has been completed, work 14 rows st.st. in feu.
Now work from Chart C, placing row 1 of chart after first 3 (4, 6, 8) sts. feu. When row 16 has been completed, work 16 rows st.st. in feu.

Shape back neck
Next row: K.28 (29, 31, 33) sts., turn and leave rem. sts. on a stitch holder.
Work on these sts. only.
*** Bind off 4 sts. at beg of next and foll. alt. row.
Bind off rem. 20 (21, 23, 25) sts.
Return to rem. sts.
With RS facing, slip first 10 sts. onto a stitch holder. Rejoin

"Giant Panda" modeled by *BA Robertson, composer and lyricist, and writer of many international hit records, the latest being* The Living Years. *He is currently producing his first film for the Walt Disney Company.*

yarn and k. to end: 28 (29, 31, 33) sts.

P. 1 row. Work from *** to end.

FRONT

Work as given for back from ** to **. Change to size 10 needles and using feu, work 4 (8, 16, 20) rows st.st.

Now work from Chart A, placing row 1 of chart after first 10 (11, 13, 15) sts. feu, until row 48 has been completed.

Shape front neck

Next row: K.32 (33, 35, 37) sts. feu, bind off 2 sts., work in pat. to end.

Next row: P.32 (33, 35, 37) sts. in pat., turn and leave rem. sts. on a stitch holder.

Work on these sts. only for right front neck.

Keeping pat. correct, ** dec 1 st. at neck edge only on next and foll. alt. rows until 20 (21, 23, 25) sts. rem. ** Work 16 rows even. Bind off.

Return to rem. sts. With WS facing, rejoin yarn at center front, p. to end.

Then work as given for right front neck from ** to **.

Work 15 rows even.

Bind off.

 Feu (05)	● Noir (16)
□ Blanc (01)	● Persan (07)

RIGHT SLEEVE

** Using size 8 needles and noir, cast on 27 (31, 31, 33) sts. Work 13 rib rows as given for back.

Inc. row: Rib 2 (4, 1, 2), m.1, * rib 3, m.1; rep from * to last 1 (3, 0, 1) sts., rib to end **: 36 (40, 42, 44) sts.

Change to size 10 needles and st.st., work 50 (54, 56, 60) rows feu, 2 rows noir, 14 rows blanc, 2 rows noir, then 2 rows feu, *** at the same time, shape sleeve by inc. 1 st. at each end of 5th and every foll. 4th row until there are 66 (68, 70, 74) sts. Then work 9 (17, 19, 19) rows even. Bind off. ***

LEFT SLEEVE

Work as given for right sleeve from ** to **.

Change to size 10 needles and work 0 (4, 6, 10) rows feu, then work Chart D, placing row 1 after first 11 (14, 15, 17) sts. feu. When row 47 has been completed, work 3 rows feu, 2 rows noir, 14 rows blanc, 2 rows noir and 2 rows feu, at the same time, shape sleeve as given for right sleeve from *** to ***.

NECKBAND

Join left shoulder seam. Using size 8 needles and feu, pick up and k.11 sts. down right back neck, k. across 10 sts. from holder, pick up and k. 12 sts. up left back neck, 43 sts. down left front and 43 sts. up right front: 119 sts.

P.1 row. Bind off.

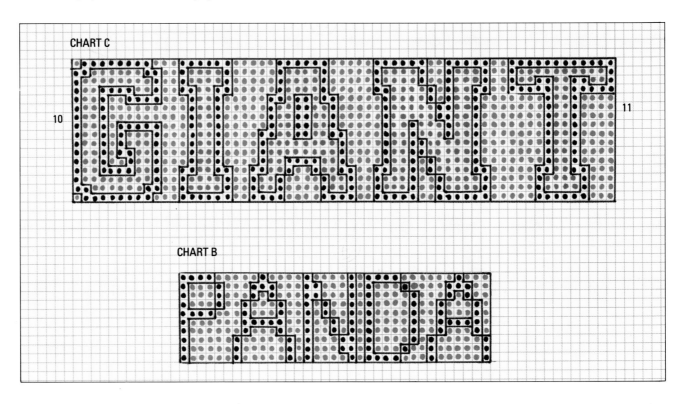

CHART C

CHART B

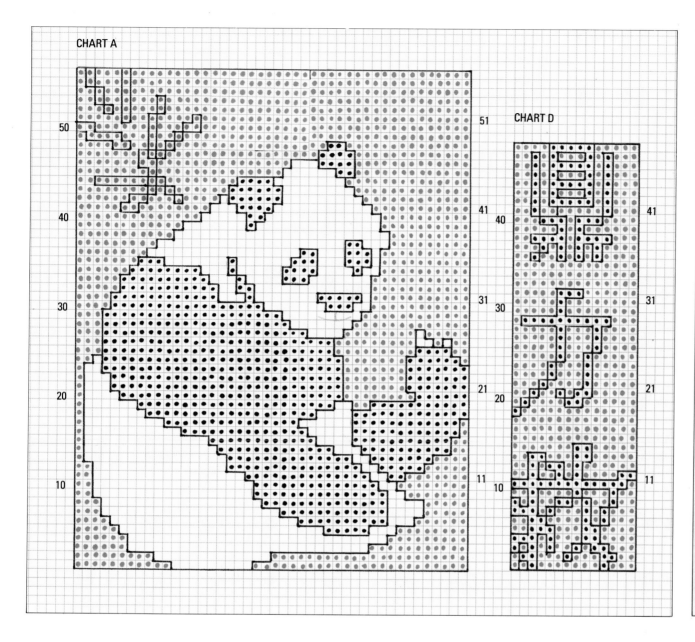

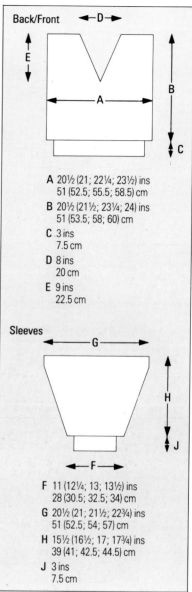

Back/Front

A 20½ (21; 22¼; 23½) ins
51 (52.5; 55.5; 58.5) cm

B 20½ (21½; 23¼; 24) ins
51 (53.5; 58; 60) cm

C .3 ins
7.5 cm

D 8 ins
20 cm

E 9 ins
22.5 cm

Sleeves

F 11 (12¼; 13; 13½) ins
28 (30.5; 32.5; 34) cm

G 20½ (21; 21½; 22¾) ins
51 (52.5; 54; 57) cm

H 15½ (16½; 17; 17¾) ins
39 (41; 42.5; 44.5) cm

J 3 ins
7.5 cm

COLLAR

Using size 8 needles and noir, cast on 119 sts.
Working in k.1, p.1 rib, work 1 row noir, then 12 rows blanc.

Shape collar

Next row: Rib to within 16 sts. of end, with yarn in front (wyif) sl.1, turn.

Next row: Wyif sl.1, rib to within 16 sts. of end, wyif sl.1, turn.

Next row: Wyif sl.1, rib to within 6 sts. of last short row, wyif sl.1, turn. Rep. last row 9 times more.

Next row: Rib to end.

Next row: Rib across all sts.

Rib 2 rows noir and then 2 rows feu. Bind off in rib.

TO FINISH

Block and press pieces lightly under a damp cloth foll. instructions. With RS tog., join right shoulder seam and neckband. With WS tog., sew bound-off edge of collar to bound-off edge of neckband. Wrap left side of collar over right side and stitch in place, folding back edge of left collar. Sew in sleeves, then join side and sleeve seams.

CHILD'S PANDA JACKET

SIZES

To fit 23½ (25, 26½, 29)in chest.

MATERIALS

Pingouin Chunky
5 (5, 5, 6) × 1¾oz balls Feu (shade 05)
2 × 1¾oz balls Noir (shade 16)
1 (2, 2, 2) × 1¾oz balls Blanc (shade 01)
1 × 1¾oz ball Persan (shade 07)
A pair each of sizes 8 and 10 knitting needles
6 × ⅝in black buttons
Stitch holder

GAUGE

13 sts. and 18 rows to 4in over motif on size 10 needles

To save time, take time to check gauge.

NOTES

Directions for larger sizes shown in parentheses ().
When working motif, use separate small balls of yarn.
When joining in a new color, leave an end of about 2in for
weaving in later and when changing color, twist yarns
together at back of work to avoid making a hole.

BACK

Using size 8 needles and noir, cast on 45 (49, 51, 55) sts.
Working in k.1, p.1 rib, work 1 row noir, 5 rows blanc, 1
row noir.
Inc. row: Using noir, rib 7 (9, 9, 11) sts., m.1, * rib 8, m.1;
rep. from * to last 6 (8, 10, 12) sts., rib to end: 50 (54, 56,
60) sts.

*"Panda" modeled by Rory
Robertson, first born of
proud mother Karen
Manners. This is his
premier modeling
assignment.*

Change to size 10 needles and using feu, work 2 (8, 14, 20) rows st.st. Now work from Chart A, placing row 1 of chart after first 2 (4, 5, 7) sts. feu, until row 54 has been completed.

Shape back neck

Following chart for colors, shape neck as follows:

Next row: K.22 (24, 25, 27), turn and leave rem. sts. on a stitch holder. Work on these sts. only.

Next row: Bind off 3 sts., p. to end.

K.1 row. Bind off 2 (2, 3, 3) sts., p. to end.

Bind off rem. 17 (19, 19, 21) sts.

Return to sts. on stitch holder.

With RS facing, slip first 6 sts. onto a stitch holder. Rejoin yarn and work to end. Now complete 2nd side of neck to match first, reversing all shaping.

LEFT FRONT

** Using size 8 needles and noir, cast on 17 (19, 21, 23) sts.

Work rib as given for back.

Inc. row: Rib 5 (5, 7, 7), m.1, * rib 4, m.1; rep from * to last 4 (6, 6, 8) sts., rib to end: 20 (22, 24, 26) sts. **

Change to size 10 needles and using feu work 8 (12, 16, 22) rows st.st. Now work from Chart E, placing row 1 of chart after first 2 (4, 6, 8) sts. feu, until row 32 has been completed. Using feu, work 2 rows st.st.

Shape front neck

*** Dec 1 st. at neck edge only on next and every foll. 4th row until 17 (19, 19, 21) sts. rem. ***

Work 9 (11, 5, 5) rows even.

Bind off.

RIGHT FRONT

Work as given for left front from ** to **.

Change to size 10 needles and using feu, work 3 (7, 11, 17) rows st.st. Now work from Chart D, placing chart after first 2 (4, 6, 8) sts feu, until row 39 has been completed.

Shape front neck

Continuing in pat. from chart, shape neck as given for left front from *** to ***.

Work 10 (12, 6, 6) rows even.

Bind off.

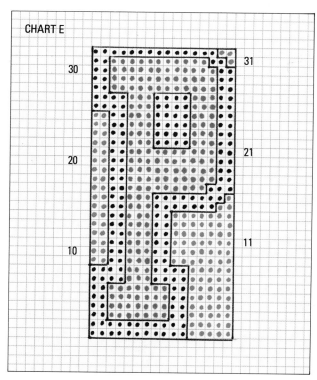

CHART E

 Feu (05)

 Blanc (01)

 Noir (16)

 Persan (07)

GIANT PANDA

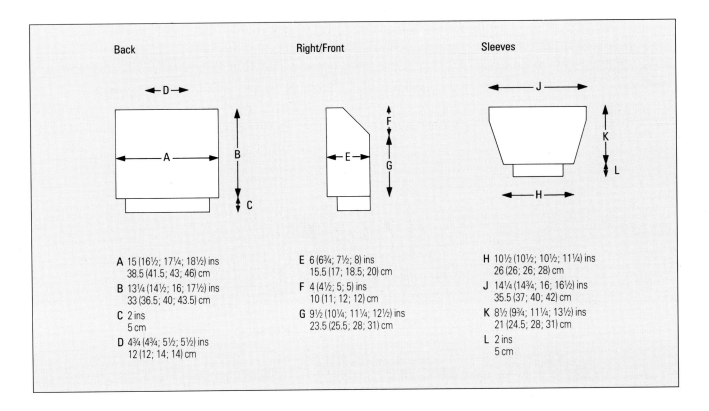

Back			

A 15 (16½; 17¼; 18½) ins
38.5 (41.5; 43; 46) cm

B 13¼ (14½; 16; 17½) ins
33 (36.5; 40; 43.5) cm

C 2 ins
5 cm

D 4¾ (4¾; 5½; 5½) ins
12 (12; 14; 14) cm

E 6 (6¾; 7½; 8) ins
15.5 (17; 18.5; 20) cm

F 4 (4½; 5; 5) ins
10 (11; 12; 12) cm

G 9½ (10¼; 11¼; 12½) ins
23.5 (25.5; 28; 31) cm

H 10½ (10½; 10½; 11¼) ins
26 (26; 26; 28) cm

J 14¼ (14¾; 16; 16½) ins
35.5 (37; 40; 42) cm

K 8½ (9¾; 11¼; 13½) ins
21 (24.5; 28; 31) cm

L 2 ins
5 cm

SLEEVES

Using size 8 needles and noir, cast on 27 (27, 27, 29) sts.
Working in k.1, p.1 rib, work 1 row noir, 5 rows blanc, 1 row noir.

Inc. row: Using noir, rib 5, m.1, * rib 3, m.1; rep from * to last 4 (4, 4, 6) sts., rib to end: 34 (34, 34, 36) sts.
Change to size 10 needles.
Using st.st., work 22 (28, 34, 40) rows feu, 2 rows noir, 10 rows blanc, 2 rows noir, and 2 rows feu at the same time, shape sleeves by inc. 1 st. at each end of 5th and every foll. 4th row until there are 46 (48, 52, 54) sts.
Work 13 (15, 13, 19) rows even.
Bind off.

RIGHT COLLAR

Join right shoulder seam.
With RS facing, using size 8 needles and feu, start at right front edge and pick up and k.57 (61, 67, 71) sts. to center back neck.
Rib 14 rows.

Shape collar

Next row: Rib 30 sts., with yarn in front sl.1, turn.
Next row: * With yarn in front sl.1, rib to end.

Next row: Rib to within 4 sts. of last short row, with yarn in front sl.1, turn. Rep. from * 3 times more.
Next row: Rib across all sts.
Bind off in rib.

LEFT COLLAR

With RS tog., join left shoulder seam.
With RS facing, using size 8 needles and feu, start at center back neck and pick up and k.57 (61, 67, 71) sts. to left front edge.
Work 2 rows in k.1, p.1 rib.
Next row: place buttonholes: ** Rib 2, yo, k.2 tog., * rib 8, yo, k.2 tog.; rep from * once, rib to end. **
Rib 7 rows, then rep from ** to ** once.
Rib 2 rows, then shape collar as given for right collar, reversing all shaping.

TO FINISH

Block and press pieces lightly under a damp cloth foll. yarn label instructions. Join collar seam at center back neck. Sew in sleeves, then join side and sleeve seams. Sew on buttons to correspond.

The Arctic may seem a harsh and forbidding place, but in fact it teems with wildlife. Seals, walruses, and whales abound in the sea; on land, mammals as diverse as lemmings, arctic foxes, reindeer, musk oxen, and polar bears are found, and many bird species migrate here to breed in the brief northern summer. Mankind has not been slow to appreciate this richness and many species have been hunted for food and, often, for their luxuriant fur. As a result some, such as polar bears and musk oxen, have become rare. However, harvest of these is now in general carefully controlled and there is little danger of their becoming extinct in the near future. A more serious long-term threat is the possibility of large-scale disruption of the environment caused by extraction of oil and minerals. Such activities will have to be controlled to ensure the beauty of the area and the preservation of its wildlife.

Arctic
POLAR BEARS AND BABY SEALS

SIZES
To fit 32 (34, 36)in chest.

MATERIALS
Pingouin Chunky
6 × 1¾oz balls Blanc (shade 01)
3 × 1¾oz balls each of Ecru (shade 10) and Jeans (shade 19)
1 × 1¾oz ball each of Noir (shade 16), Nuage (shade 12), and Souris (17)
5 × ¾in buttons, 1 × ¼in clear plastic snap.
A pair each of sizes 6 and 10 knitting needles
Stitch holder

GAUGE
16 sts. and 22 rows to 4in over pat. worked on size 7 needles

To save time, take time to check gauge.

NOTES
Directions for larger sizes are given in parentheses ().
When working motif, use separate, small balls of yarn. When joining in a new color, leave an end of about 2in for weaving in later. When changing color, twist yarns together at back of work to avoid making a hole.

BACK
Using size 6 needles and blanc, cast on 85 (89, 93) sts.
Rib row 1: K.1, * p.1, k.1; rep. from * to end.
Rib row 2: P.1, * k.1, p.1; rep. from * to end.
Rep. 2 rib rows 3 times more, inc. 1 st. at beg. of last row: 86 (90, 94) sts.
Change to size 7 needles and work from row 1 of Chart A.
Shape armholes by binding off 8 sts. at beg. of rows 31 and 32, then cont. working even until row 72 has been completed: 70 (74, 78) sts.

Shape back neck
Next row: K.25 (27, 29), turn and leave rem. sts. on a stitch holder.
Work on these sts. only.
Next row: Bind off 3 sts., p. to end.
K.1 row.
Next row: Bind off 2 sts., p. to end.
Bind off rem. 20 (22, 24) sts.

> This cozy jacket really captures the feel of the Arctic. The allover design shows masterful males, a female with suckling cubs and on the sleeves, young bears at rest and play. The coal-black features are in sharp contrast to the soft, creamy hues of their coats and the crispness of the white snow and blue sky. Diamanté buttons complete the icy look.

POLAR BEARS

"Polar Bears" modeled by Angie Rutherford, wife of Mike. She is a keen horsewoman.

Return to rem. sts.

With RS facing, slip first 20 sts. onto a stitch holder, rejoin yarn to first st. and k. to end. Complete 2nd side of back neck to match first side, reversing all shaping.

RIGHT FRONT

Using size 6 needles and blanc, cast on 49 (51, 53) sts. Work 2 rows rib as given for back.

Rib row 3: Rib 2, bind off 2 sts., rib to end.

Rib row 4: Rib to buttonhole, cast on 2 sts., rib 2. Starting rib row 1, work 3 rows rib.

Rib row 8: P.1, m.1, rib to last 7 sts., turn and leave rem. 7 sts. on a stitch holder.

Change to size 7 needles and work from row 1 of Chart B, shaping armhole as given for back at beg. of row 32: 41 (43, 45) sts.

Cont. until row 61 (63, 65) has been completed.

□	Blanc (01)
□	Ecru (10)
▨	Jeans (19)
◉	Souris (17)
◉	Nuage (12)
●	Noir (16)

CHART A

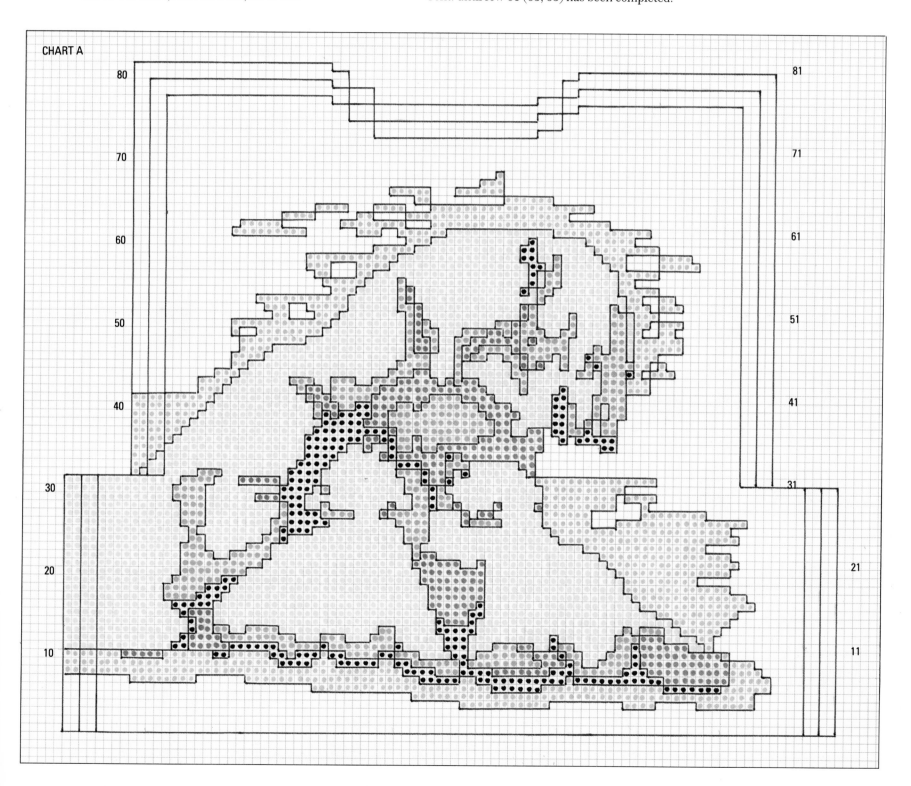

POLAR BEARS

CHART C

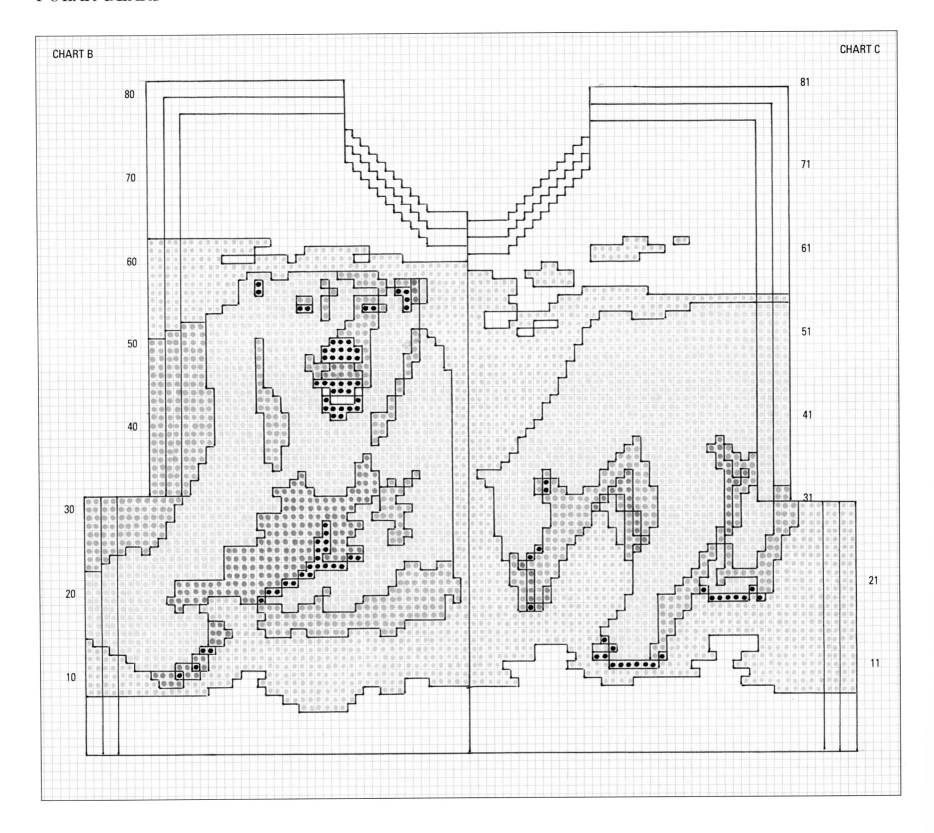

CHART D

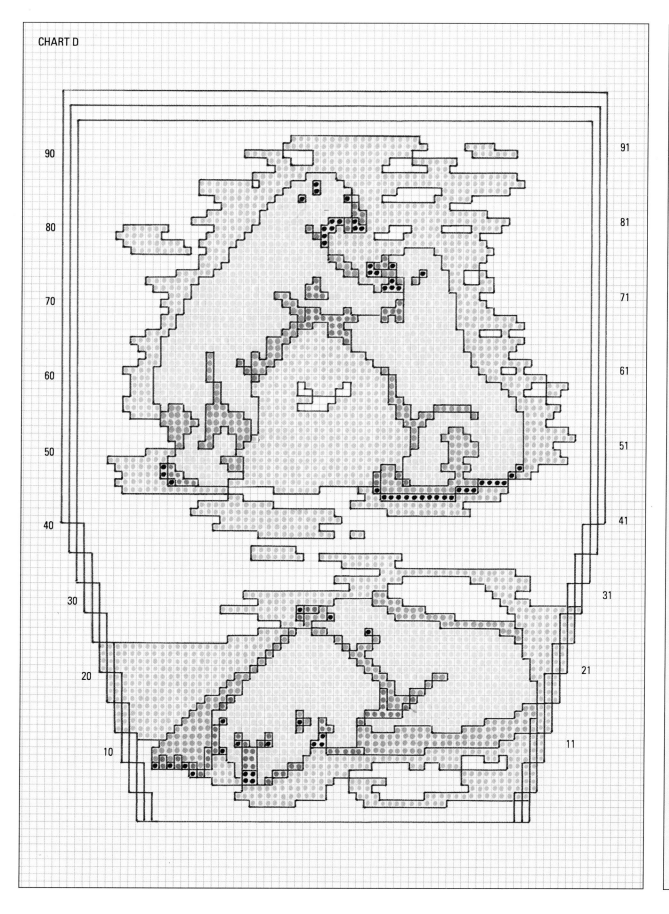

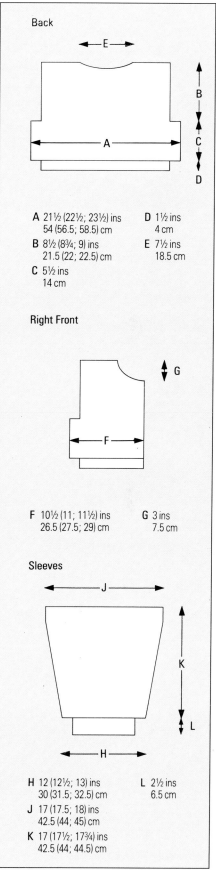

Back

E

B

A

C

D

A 21½ (22½; 23½) ins
54 (56.5; 58.5) cm

D 1½ ins
4 cm

B 8½ (8¾; 9) ins
21.5 (22; 22.5) cm

E 7½ ins
18.5 cm

C 5½ ins
14 cm

Right Front

G

F

F 10½ (11; 11½) ins
26.5 (27.5; 29) cm

G 3 ins
7.5 cm

Sleeves

J

K

L

H

H 12 (12½; 13) ins
30 (31.5; 32.5) cm

L 2½ ins
6.5 cm

J 17 (17.5; 18) ins
42.5 (44; 45) cm

K 17 (17½; 17¾) ins
42.5 (44; 44.5) cm

Shape front neck

Next row: P. to last 7 sts., p.2 tog., turn and leave rem. 5 sts. on a stitch holder.

Work on these sts. only.

** Dec. 1 st. at neck edge only on every row until 20 (22, 24) sts. rem.

Work 5 rows even. Bind off. **

LEFT FRONT

Using size 6 needles and blanc, cast on 49 (51, 53) sts.

Work 8 rows in rib as given for back, inc. 1 st. at end of last row: 50 (52, 54) sts.

Change to size 7 needles and k. to last 7 sts., turn and leave rem. 7 sts. on a stitch holder.

Work on these sts. only from row 2 of Chart C, shaping armhole as given for back at beg. of row 31: 42 (44, 46) sts.

Cont. until row 60 has been completed.

Shape left front neck

Next row: K. to last 5 sts., turn and leave rem. 5 sts. on a stitch holder.

Work on these sts. only.

Work as given for right front from ** to **.

SLEEVES

Using size 6 needles and blanc, cast on 37 (39, 41) sts.

Work in rib as given for back for 2½in, ending rib row 1.

Inc. row: Rib 3 (5, 5), m.1, * rib 3, m.1; rep. from * to last 4 (4, 6) sts., rib to end: 48 (50, 52) sts.

Change to size 7 needles and work from row 1 of Chart D.

Shape sleeves by inc. 1 st. each end of 5th and every foll. 4th row until there are 68 (70, 72) sts.

Work even until row 94 (96, 98) has been completed from Chart D. Bind off.

BUTTONBAND

Return to 7 sts. on stitch holder on left front.

Using size 6 needles and blanc, with RS facing, join yarn to first st. and work 60 (62, 64) rows rib as set.

Leave these sts. on a stitch holder.

Stitch buttonband to left front matching row by row.

BUTTONHOLE BAND

Return to 7 sts. on stitch holder on right front. Using size 6 needles and blanc, with WS facing, join yarn to first st.

** Work in rib as set until 18 rows have been worked from last buttonhole, then work 2 rows for buttonhole.**

Work from ** to ** twice more (4 buttonholes made).

Work 4 rows rib, leave these sts. on a stitch holder. Stitch buttonhole band to right front, matching row by row.

COLLAR

Join shoulder seams.

Using size 6 needles and blanc, with RS facing and starting at right front, rib across 7 sts. from buttonhole band as set, k. across 5 sts. from stitch holder, pick up and k.19 sts. up right front neck, 11 sts. down right back neck, k. across 20 sts. from stitch holder, pick up and k.12 sts. up left back neck, 19 sts. down left front, k. across 5 sts. from stitch holder and rib 7 sts. from buttonband as set: 105 sts.

Row 1: Rib 7, p. to last 7 sts., rib 7.

Starting rib row 1 as given for back, work 6 (4, 2) rows rib.

Dec. row: Rib 8, k.3 tog., rib to last 11 sts., sl.1, k.2 tog., psso, rib 8: 101 sts.

Starting rib row 2 as given for back, work 5 rows rib.

Buttonhole row: Rib 2, bind off 2 sts., rib 3, k.3 tog., rib to last 11 sts., sl.1, k.2 tog., psso, rib 8.

Next row: Rib to buttonhole, cast on 2 sts., rib to end: 97 sts.

Starting rib row 1 as given for back, rib 3 (5, 7) rows.

Bind off.

TO FINISH

Block and press pieces lightly under a damp cloth foll. yarn label instructions. Joining bound-off edge of armhole to underarms, sew in sleeves, then join side and sleeve seams. Sew on buttons. Sew snap to top of front opening.

BABY SEALS

SIZES

To fit 18 (19, 20, 22)in chest.

Age 0–6 (6–12, 12–18, 24) months

MATERIALS

Patons Beehive Soft Blend medium-weight

Sweater

2 (3, 3, 4) × 1¾oz balls Cornflower (shade 6977)

1 × 1¾oz balls each of White (shade 6963), Gray (6984),

Black (6955), and Silver Gray (6962)

Leggings

2 × 1¾oz balls White (shade 6963)

1 × 1¾oz balls each of Cornflower (shade 6977) and Gray

(6984)

A pair each of sizes 3 and 4 knitting needles

3 × ½in buttons

Round elastic to fit waist

GAUGE

24 sts. and 31 rows to 4in over pat. worked on size 4
needles

To save time, take time to check gauge.

NOTES

Directions for larger sizes are given in parentheses ().
When working motif, use separate, small balls of yarn.
When joining in a new color, leave an end of about 2in for
weaving in later, and when changing color, twist yarns
together at back of work to avoid making a hole.

BACK

** Using size 3 needles and cornflower, cast on 60 (62, 64,
72) sts.

Rib row: *K.1, p.1; rep. from * to end.

Rep rib row for 1½in, ending with an RS row.

Inc. row: Rib 7 (9, 9, 5), m.1, * rib 9, m.1; rep. from * to last
8 (8, 10, 4) sts., rib to end: 66 (68, 70, 80) sts. **

Change to size 4 needles and work 6 (8, 10, 16) rows
st.st.

*"Baby Seals" modeled by
Harry Rutherford, new-born
of Angie Rutherford.*

Next row: K.13 (14, 15, 20) sts., work row 1 from Chart A,
k.14 (15, 16, 21) sts.

Cont. even until row 74 has been completed from Chart.

3rd and 4th sizes only

Using cornflower, work 4 (8) rows st.st.

All sizes

Cont. for all sizes as follows:

Shape back neck

Next row: K.26 (27, 27, 32) sts., turn and leave rem. sts. on
a stitch holder.

▶ Crisp, blue color
provides a perfect
backdrop for these cute Seal
cubs. Reproduced in
beautiful detail, the softness
is created with gray hues. A
simple snowflake jacquard on
the back and sleeves and
three-button neck opening
complete the design.

BABY SEALS

Work on these sts. only.

Next row: Bind off 4 sts., p. to end.

K.1 row.

Next row: Bind off 2 sts., p. to end.

Bind off.

With RS facing, slip first 14 (14, 16, 16) sts. onto a stitch holder.

Rejoin yarn and K. to end.

Work 2nd side of back neck to match first side, reversing all shaping.

Bind off.

FRONT

Work as given for back from ** to **. Change to size 4 needles and work 17 (19, 25, 31) rows st.st.

Now work rows 1–45 (45, 47, 49) from Chart B (note: row 1 is a p. row).

Shape front neck

Next row: Working in pat., k.27 (28, 29, 34) sts., turn and leave rem. sts. on a stitch holder.

Work on these sts. only.

Cornflower (6977)

White (6963)

Gray (6984)

Silver Gray (6962)

Black (6955)

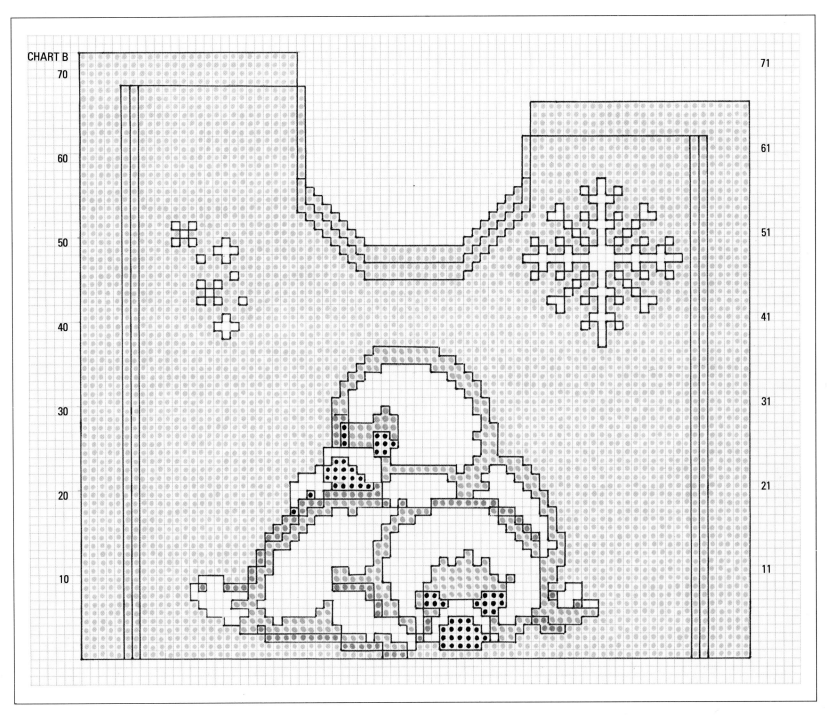

Dec. 1 st. at neck edge only on every row until 19 (20, 22, 26) sts. rem.

Work 8 (8, 7, 8) rows even.

Bind off.

With RS facing, slip first 12 sts. onto a stitch holder, rejoin yarn and k. to end.

Dec. 1 st. at neck edge only on every row until 19 (20, 22, 26) sts. rem.

Work 14 (14, 13,14) rows even.

Bind off.

SLEEVES

Using size 3 needles and cornflower, cast on 36 (36, 38, 40) sts. Rep. rib row as given for back for 1¼in, ending with an RS row.

Inc. row: Rib 5 (5, 6, 7), m.1, * rib 3, m.1; rep. from * to last 4 (4, 5, 6) sts., rib to end: 46 (46, 48, 50) sts.

Change to size 4 needles and work from row 19 (1, 1, 1) of Chart C. Shape sides by inc. 1 st. at each end of 7th, then every foll. 6th row until there are 54 (58, 62, 56) sts, then every foll. 4th row until there are 60 (64, 68, 74) sts.

Work 3 rows even.

Bind off.

NECKBAND

Join right shoulder seam.

Using size 3 needles and cornflower, with RS facing, pick up and k.16 (16, 17, 17) sts. down left front neck, k. across 12 sts. from holder, pick up and k.22 (22, 23, 23) sts. up right front neck, pick up and k.8 sts. down right back neck, k. across 14 (14, 16, 16) sts. from holder, pick up and k.9 sts. up left back neck: 81 (81, 85, 85) sts.

P.1 row.

Rib row 1: K.1, * p.1, k.1; rep. from * to end.

Rib row 2: P.1 * k.1, p.1; rep. from * to end.

Rep. 2 rib rows twice more.

Bind off in rib.

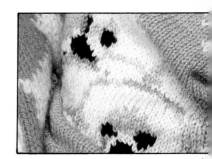

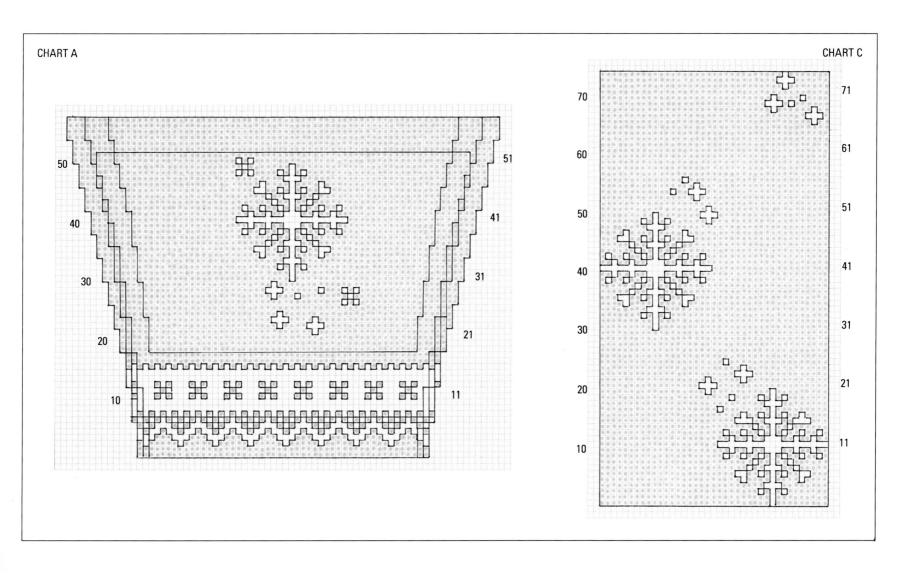

BUTTONBAND

With RS facing, using size 3 needles and cornflower, pick up and k.29 (31, 31, 37) sts. across neckband and left back shoulder. P.1 row.

Rep. 2 rib rows as given for neckband 3 times.

Bind off in rib.

BUTTONHOLE BAND

With RS facing, using size 3 needles and cornflower, pick up and k.29 (31, 31, 37) sts. across left front shoulder and neckband edge. P.1 row.

Rep. 2 rib rows as given for neckband, once.

Next row: Rib 3, * yo, rib 2 tog., rib 9 (10, 10, 11); rep. from * once, yo, rib 2 tog., rib 2 (2, 2, 6).

Starting with rib row 2, work 3 rows in k.1, p.1 rib as given for neckband.

Bind off in rib.

TO FINISH

Lap buttonhole band over buttonband and stitch together at armhole edge. Block and press pieces lightly under a damp cloth foll. yarn label instructions. Sew in sleeves. Join side and sleeve seams. Sew on buttons to correspond with buttonholes.

LEGGINGS (Make 2)

Using size 4 needles and cornflower, cast on 64 (68, 72, 86) sts.

Work in k.1, p.1 rib as given for sweater back in the foll. colors: 2 rows cornflower, 2 rows white, 2 rows gray, 2 rows white.

Rep. 8 row stripe pat. throughout and at the same time, inc. 1 st. at each end of every 2nd (4th, 4th, 4th) row 20 (5, 11, 19) times, then every foll. alt row 4 (19, 13, 5) times, taking new sts. into rib: 112 (116, 120, 134) sts.

Cont. until work measures 7 (8¼, 9¾, 11¾)in from beg.

Shape top of leg

Bind off 3 sts. at beg. of next 2 rows, 2 sts. at beg. of foll. 2 rows, then 1 st. at each end of next row: 100 (104, 108, 122) sts. Cont. even until work measures 12¾ (14½, 16½, 18½)in, ending with 2nd row white.

Shape waist

(Work short rows)

1st row: Rib 66 (69, 72, 81) sts., with yarn in front (wyif) sl.1, turn.

2nd row: Wyif sl.1, ybk, rib to end.

3rd row: Rib 44 (46, 48, 54) sts., wyif sl.1, turn.

4th row: As 2nd.

5th row: Rib 22, (23, 24, 27) sts., wyif sl.1, turn.

6th row: As 2nd.

Now work 2 rows white across all sts.

Change to size 3 needles and using cornflower, work 4 cm in k.1, p.1 rib. Bind off in rib.

TO FINISH

Turn one leg to wrong side in order to match short row stripes at center back. Join center back and front seams. Join leg seams, reversing seam for last 1¼in for ankle cuff. Thread elastic through waistband.

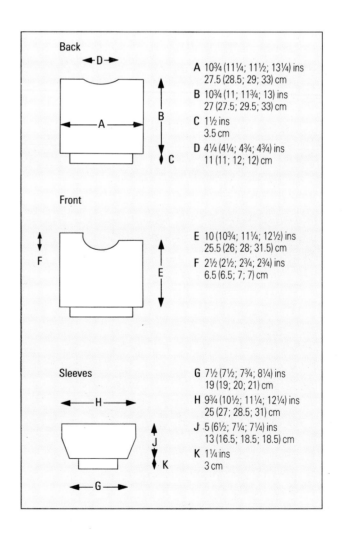

A	10¾ (11¼; 11½; 13¼) ins 27.5 (28.5; 29; 33) cm
B	10¾ (11; 11¾; 13) ins 27 (27.5; 29.5; 33) cm
C	1½ ins 3.5 cm
D	4¼ (4¼; 4¾; 4¾) ins 11 (11; 12; 12) cm
E	10 (10¾; 11¼; 12½) ins 25.5 (26; 28; 31.5) cm
F	2½ (2½; 2¾; 2¾) ins 6.5 (6.5; 7; 7) cm
G	7½ (7½; 7¾; 8¼) ins 19 (19; 20; 21) cm
H	9¾ (10½; 11¼; 12¼) ins 25 (27; 28.5; 31) cm
J	5 (6½; 7¼; 7¼) ins 13 (16.5; 18.5; 18.5) cm
K	1¼ ins 3 cm

Much loved by people throughout the world, Elephants are coming under increasing threat in their natural habitat. Between 30,000 and 40,000 of the rarer Asian Elephant currently survive in the forests of South and South-east Asia, although this number is constantly decreasing as these forests are logged or cleared for agriculture. The only places where Asian Elephants are at all secure are a few large national parks such as Taman Negara in Malaysia. By far the biggest threat to the African Elephant is poaching for ivory. Despite legal protection in many countries and international controls on ivory trade, tens of thousands of Elephants are killed each year and the ivory smuggled abroad. The overall population has dropped from an estimated 1,250,000 in the late 1970s to fewer than 750,000 today. Fortunately, some countries, most notably Zimbabwe, are working hard to conserve their Elephant populations.

African ELEPHANTS *Mother and Calf*

SIZES
To fit 27 (30, 32, 33)in chest.
Age 7 (9, 11, 13) years.

MATERIALS
Pingouin France + medium weight
2 (2, 3, 3) × 50g balls Persan (shade 13)
2 × 50g balls Turquoise (shade 14)
2 (2, 3, 3) × 50g balls Soleil (shade 10)
1 × 50g balls each of Souris (shade 19),
Blanc (01), Perle (18) and Noir (20)
A pair each of 3mm (No. 11) and 3¾mm (No. 9) knitting needles
Stitch holder

GAUGE
24 sts. and 28 rows to 4in over pat. worked on size 5 needles

To save time, take time to check gauge.

NOTES
Directions for larger sizes are given in parentheses ().
When working motif, use separate, small balls of yarn.
When joining in a new color, leave an end of about 2in for weaving in later. When changing color, twist yarns together at back of work to avoid making a hole.

BACK
** Using size 3 needles and persan, cast on 90 (96, 100, 104) sts.
Rib row: * K.1, p.1; rep. from * to end.
Rep. rib row for 2½in, ending with an RS row.
Inc. row: Rib 10 (13, 15, 17), m.1, * rib 14, m.1; rep. from * to last 10 (13, 15, 17) sts., rib to end: 96 (102, 106, 110) sts.
Change to size 5 needles and work 21 (25, 29, 35) rows st.st. **
Work rows 1–41 from Chart A (note: row 1 is a p. row).

Shape armholes
Bind off 4 (5, 6, 6) sts. at beg. of next 2 rows: 88 (92, 94, 98) sts. Cont. working even until row 85 (87, 91, 93) has been completed.

Shape back neck
Next row: K.32 (33, 33, 34), turn and leave rem. sts. on a spare needle.
Work on these sts. only.
Next row: Bind off 5 sts., p. to end.

▶ This colorful child's sweater features the front and rear view of a female and her cub. Reproduction of an authentic National Park road sign provides color. It is again used in a neat collar which completes the design.

K.1 row.

Next row: Bind off 4 sts., p. to end.

Bind off.

Return to rem. sts.

With RS facing, slip first 24 (26, 28, 30) sts. onto a stitch holder.

Rejoin yarn to first st. and k. to end.

Complete 2nd side of back neck to match first, reversing all shaping.

FRONT

Work as given for back from ** to **, then work rows 1–41 from Chart B (note: row 1 is a p. row).

Shape armholes

Bind off 4 (5, 6, 6) sts. at beg. of next 2 rows: 88 (92, 94, 98) sts.

Cont. working even until row 75 (77, 81, 83) has been completed.

Shape front neck

Next row: K.32 (33, 33, 34) sts., turn and leave rem. sts. on a stitch holder.

Work on these sts. only.

Dec. 1 st. at neck edge only on every row until 23 (24, 24, 25) sts. rem.

Work 4 rows even. Bind off.

Return to rem. sts.

With RS facing, slip first 24 (26, 28, 30) sts. onto a stitch holder. Rejoin yarn to first st. and k. to end.

Complete 2nd side of front neck to match first, reversing all shaping.

SLEEVES

** Using size 3 needles and turquoise, cast on 45 (49, 51, 55) sts. Work 2½in of k.1, p.1 rib, ending with a RS row.

Inc. row: Rib 1 (3, 1, 3), m.1, * rib 3, m.1; rep. from * to last 2 (4, 2, 4) sts., rib to end: 60 (64, 68, 72) sts.

Change to size 5 needles and work from row 13 (7, 3, 1) of Chart C for left sleeve or Chart D for right sleeve, at the same time, shape sleeve by inc. 1 st. at each end of 5th and every foll. 6th row until there are 82 (86, 92, 96) sts.

Work even until row 96 (96, 98, 100) of chart has been completed.

Bind off.

"African Elephants"
modeled by Kate
Rutherford, eldest and only
daughter of the Rutherford
Brood.

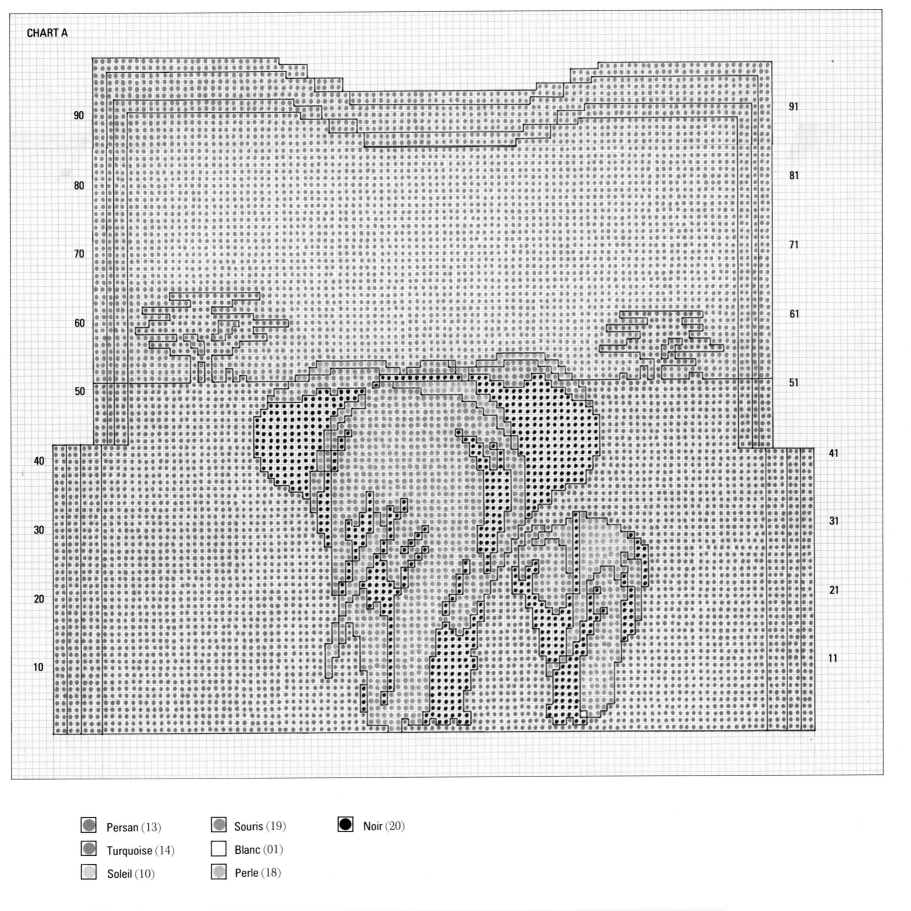

CHART A

Persan (13)   Souris (19)   Noir (20)
Turquoise (14)   Blanc (01)
Soleil (10)   Perle (18)

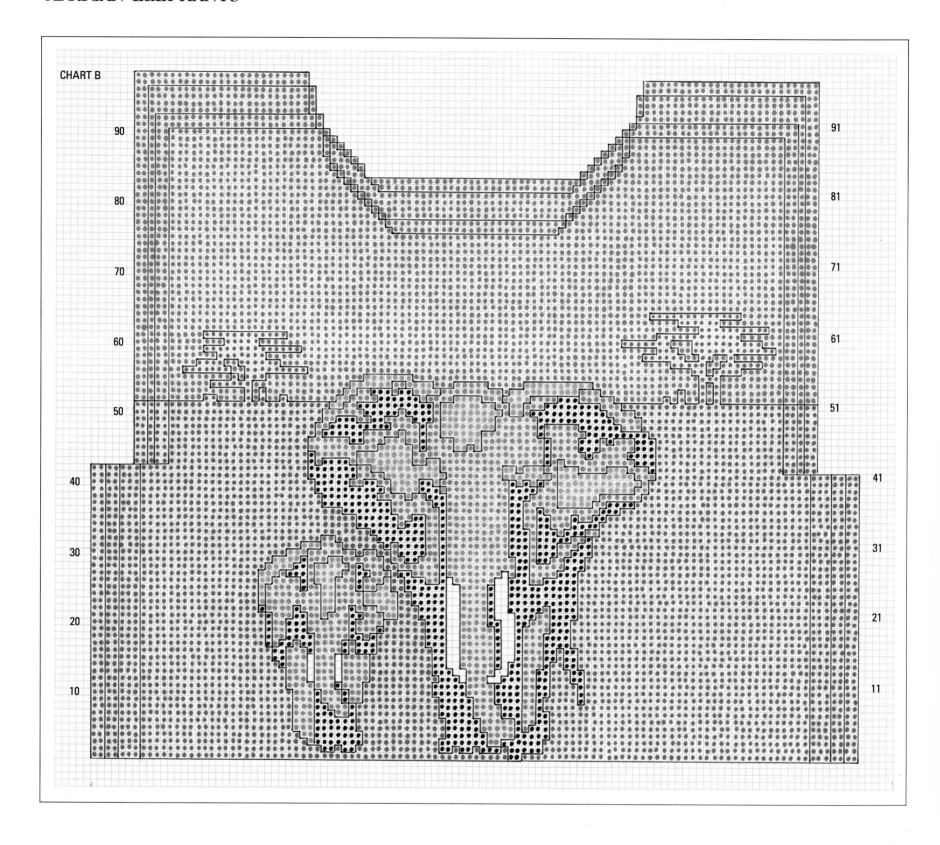

CHART B

CHART C

NECKBAND

Join left shoulder.

Using size 3 needles and turquoise and with RS facing, pick up and k.13 sts. down right back neck, k. across 24 (26, 28, 30) sts. from holder, pick up and k.14 sts. up left back neck, 16 sts. down left front neck, k. across 12 (13, 14, 15) sts. from holder, place center front marker, k. across 12 (13, 14, 15) sts. from holder, then pick up and k.16 sts. up right front neck: 107 (111, 115, 119) sts.

P.1 row.

Work 5 rows in k.1, p.1 rib.

Bind off in rib.

AFRICAN ELEPHANTS

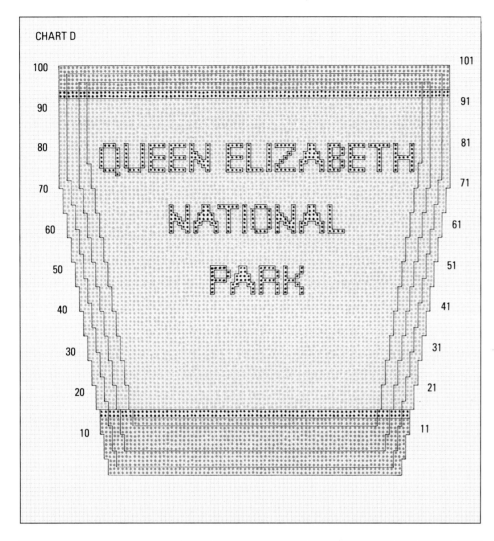

CHART D

QUEEN ELIZABETH
NATIONAL
PARK

COLLAR

Using size 3 needles and noir, cast on 107 (111, 115, 119) sts.

Working in k.1, p.1 rib, work 1 row noir, 22 rows soleil, 1 row turquoise. Using turquoise, bind off in rib.

TO FINISH

Block and press pieces lightly under a damp cloth foll. yarn label instructions. Join right shoulder and neckband seam. Starting at center front marker, stitch bound-off edge of collar to inside edge of neckband base, stitch by stitch. Join edges of collar at center front for ½in. Joining bound-off edge of armhole to underarms, sew in sleeves, then join side and sleeve seams.

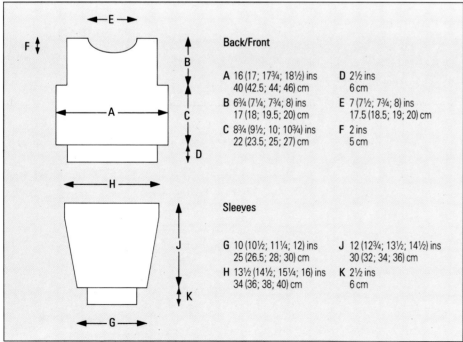

Back/Front

A 16 (17; 17¾; 18½) ins
40 (42.5; 44; 46) cm

B 6¾ (7¼; 7¾; 8) ins
17 (18; 19.5; 20) cm

C 8¾ (9½; 10; 10¾) ins
22 (23.5; 25; 27) cm

D 2½ ins
6 cm

E 7 (7½; 7¾; 8) ins
17.5 (18.5; 19; 20) cm

F 2 ins
5 cm

Sleeves

G 10 (10½; 11¼; 12) ins
25 (26.5; 28; 30) cm

H 13½ (14½; 15¼; 16) ins
34 (36; 38; 40) cm

J 12 (12¾; 13½; 14½) ins
30 (32; 34; 36) cm

K 2½ ins
6 cm

Looking like a relic from a prehistoric era, the Black Rhinoceros is in grave danger of following the mammoths and dinosaurs into the history books. Twenty years ago there were around 70,000 of them, in central, eastern, and southern Africa. Now there are fewer than 3,000 and the number is dropping fast. The sole reason for this is the Rhino's horn, which can command high prices both in the Yemen Arab Republic, where it is used to make much *sought-after dagger handles, and in the Far East where it is used in traditional medicines for treating fevers. Groups of heavily armed poachers have swept through Africa wiping out entire Rhino populations in their pursuit of the horn, often fighting pitch battles with wildlife guards and rangers in the process. The only hope of saving the last few viable populations, such as the one in the Zambezi valley in Zimbabwe, is to put a complete halt to the trade in the horn.*

Black
RHINO

SIZE
One size to fit 32–40in chest.

MATERIALS
Pingouin Chunky
13 × 1¾oz balls Beige (shade 11)
2 × 1¾oz balls Noir (shade 16)
1 × 1¾oz balls each of Blanc (shade 01), Nuage (12), and Souris (17)
Pingouin Mohican, (flecked bulky)
4 × 1¾oz balls Souris (shade 11)
Pingouin Sweet′ hair
1 × 1¾oz ball Prune (shade 14)
A pair each of sizes 8 and 10 knitting needles
Stitch holder

GAUGE
14 sts. and 16 rows to 4in over pat. size 10 needles

To save time, take time to check gauge.

NOTES
When working motif, use separate small balls of yarn.
When joining in a new color, leave an end of about 2in for weaving in later. When changing color, twist yarns together at back of work to avoid making a hole.

BACK
** Using size 8 needles and beige, cast on 69 sts.
Rib row 1: K.1, * p.1, k.1; rep. from * to end.
Rib row 2: P.1, * k.1, p.1; rep. from * to end.
Rep. these 2 rows for 3½in, ending rib row 1.
Inc. row: Rib 5, m.1, * rib 6, m.1; rep. from * to last 4 sts., rib 4: 80 sts. **
Change to size 10 needles and work 22 rows st.st.
Now work rows 1–7 from Chart A, placing chart after first 23 sts. Work 4 rows st.st., then work rows 1–7 from Chart B, placing chart after first 25 sts. Work 16 rows st.st.

Shape raglans
Bind off 2 sts. at beg. of next 2 rows, then dec. 1 st. at each end of next row: 74 sts.
P.1 row, then work rows 1–12 from Chart C, dec. 1 st. at each end of rows 1, 3, 5, 8 and 11, placing first row of chart after first 15 sts: 64 sts.
Work 6 rows st.st., dec. 1 st. at each end of 2nd and 5th rows: 60 sts.
Change to souris (shade 11) and work rows 1–12 from

► Standing strong and powerful, the distinctive shapes of the Black Rhinos are worked in intarsia knitting. Simple embroidery added in a contrasting yarn represents sun-scorched grass. Bulky yarn is used and the look is completed with garter stitch shoulders and a tight roll-neck.

Chart D, dec. 1 st. at each end of rows 2, 5, 8, and 11, placing first row of chart after first 9 sts.; 52 sts.

Using souris (shade 11), p.1 row, then dec. 1 st. at each end of every row until 30 sts. rem.

Shape back neck

Next row: K.2 tog., k.9, turn and leave rem. sts. on a spare needle. Work on these 10 sts. only.

Cont. dec. 1 st. at raglan edge on every row, at the same time, bind off 3 sts. at beg. of next and foll. alt. row.

Bind off rem. 1 st. Return to sts. on spare needle.

With RS facing, slip first 8 sts. onto a stitch holder, rejoin yarn to first st., k. to last 2 sts., k.2 tog.

Complete 2nd side of back neck to match first side, reversing all shaping.

FRONT

Work as given for back from ** to **.

Change to size 10 needles and work rows 1–92 from Chart E, shaping armholes at row 57 and raglans as indicated on chart: 46 sts.

Shape front neck

Next row: K.2 tog., k.16, turn and leave rem. sts. on a stitch holder.

Work on these sts. only.

Dec. 1 st. at each end of every row until 9 sts. rem.

Then dec. at raglan edge only on every row until 2 sts. rem. Bind off.

Return to sts. on stitch holder.

With RS facing, slip first 10 sts. onto a stitch holder, rejoin yarn to first st. and k. to last 2 sts., k.2 tog.

Complete 2nd side of front neck to match first side, reversing all shaping.

"Black Rhino" modeled by accomplished stage and TV actor Paul Nicholas. Originally a singer, he has starred in many West End musicals, including, Hair, Mutiny on the Bounty, *and* Cats. *He has been involved with the WWF on previous occasions.*

SLEEVES

Using 5mm needles and beige, cast on 31 sts.

Rep. 2 rib rows as given for back for 7.5cm, ending with rib row 1.

Inc. row: Rib 1, m.1, * rib 3, m.1; rep. from * to end: 42 sts.

Change to 6mm needles and proceed in st.st., inc. 1 st. at each end of 5th and every foll. 6th row until there are 60 sts.

Work 15 rows without shaping.

Shape raglans

Cast off 2 sts. at beg. of next 2 rows, then dec. 1 st. at each end of every row until 28 sts. rem.

Change to souris (11) and proceed in garter st., dec. 1 st. at each end of next and every foll. alt. row until 18 sts. rem. Then dec. 1 st. at each end of every foll. 4th row until 8 sts. rem. P.1 row.

Right sleeve only

Cast off 3 sts. at beg. of next and foll. alt. row. P.1 row. Cast off rem. 2 sts.

Left sleeve only

K.1 row. Cast off 3 sts. at beg. of next and foll. alt. row. Cast off rem. 2 sts.

Beige (11)
Noir (16)
Souris (11)
Blanc (01)
Nuage (12)
Souris (17)

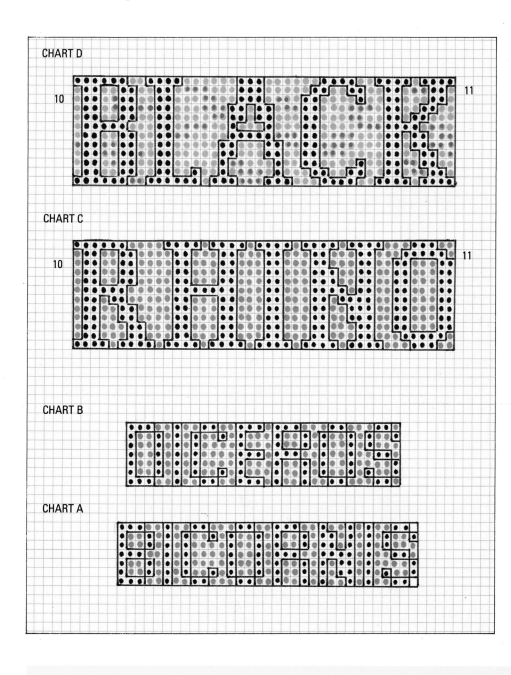

BLACK RHINO

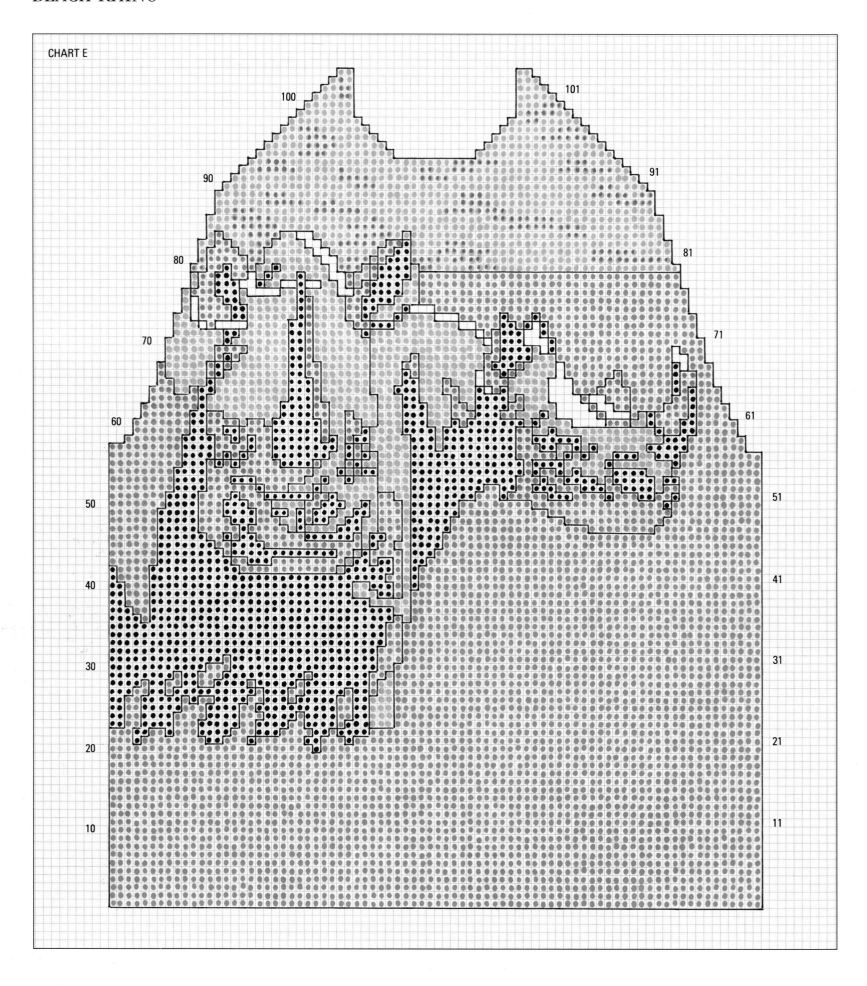

NECKBAND

Join both front and the left back raglan seams.
Using size 8 needles and souris (11), with RS facing, pick up and k.11 sts. down right back neck, k.8 sts. from holder, pick up and k.12 sts. up left back neck, 8 sts. across left sleeve, 14 sts. down left front neck, k.10 sts. from holder, pick up and k.14 sts. up right front neck, 8 sts. across right sleeve: 85 sts. P.1 row.
Bind off.

COLLAR

Using size 8 needles and souris (11), cast on 85 sts.
Rep. 2 rib rows as given for back for 16 rows.
Bind off in rib.

TO FINISH

Block and press pieces lightly under a damp cloth foll. yarn label instructions. With WS tog., backstitch bound-off edge of collar to neckband, st. by st. Join right raglan and collar seam. Join side and underarm seams. Using Sweet' hair embroider "grass" in backstitch as shown on Chart E.

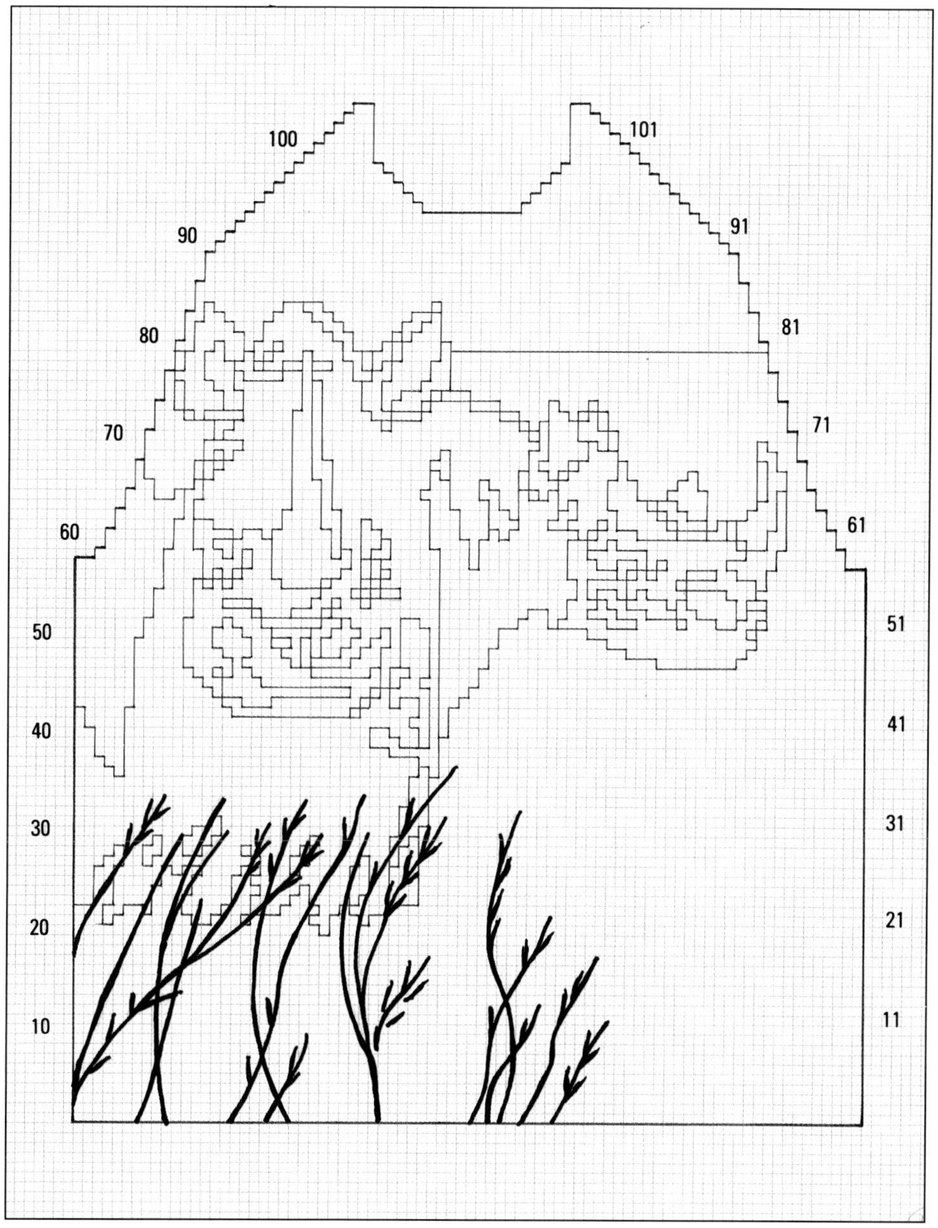

Backstitch embroidery using prune (14)

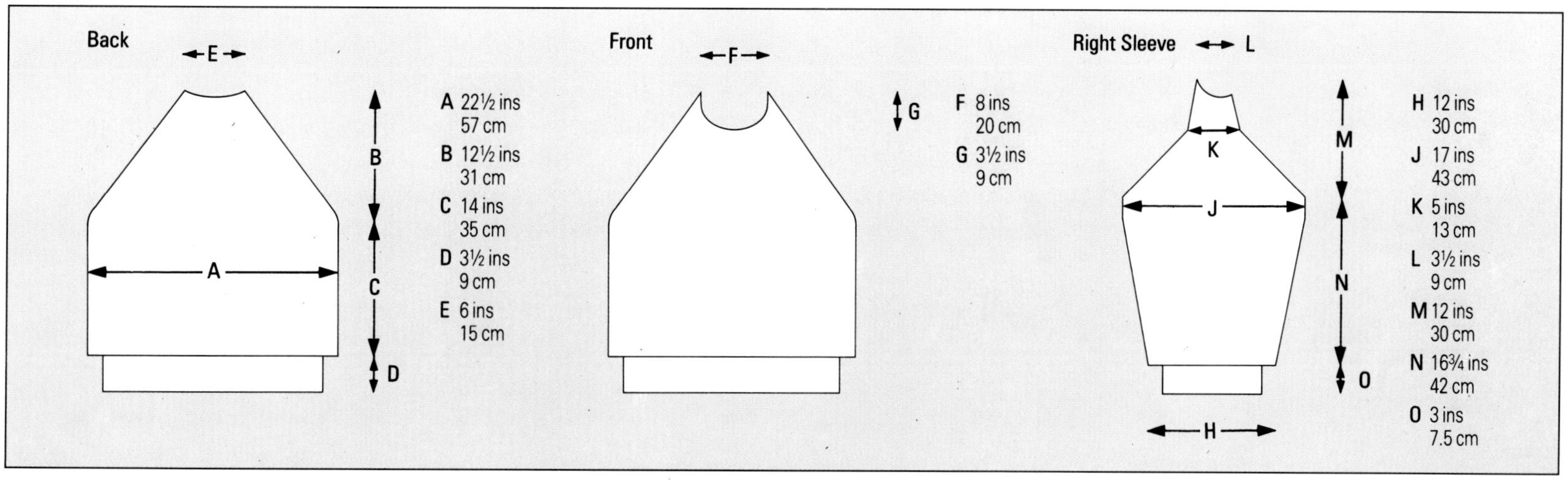

Symbols of might, Lions are still found in many parts of Africa. In the last hundred years they have been exterminated in both the far north of their range, in the Atlas Mountains of Morocco and Algeria, and the far south, in Cape Province in South Africa. Lions were also once found in the Middle East, India, and even in southern Europe. The last Lions in Europe were exterminated around 2,000 years ago, although in the Middle East they survived well into the nineteenth century. Today, however, the only wild Lions outside Africa live in the Gir Forest in north-east India where around 150 are closely protected in a wildlife sanctuary. Many African Lions are also protected in national parks and game reserves, where they are immensely popular tourist attractions, but outside these areas they are often killed for preying on domestic livestock and the population as a whole is probably decreasing.

LIONESSES
Sleeping in Acacia tree

A languorous mood is captured in this three-dimensional design. The dead acacia is twisted and knotted; the Lionesses take advantage of the sculptured limbs for slumber. A section of the main garment is translated into a junior version.

SIZES

Adult: One size to fit 32–40in chest.
Child: To fit 25 (27, 30, 32, 33) in chest. Age 5 (7, 9, 11, 13) years.

MATERIALS

Emu Superwash medium-weight 100% wool
Adult
11 × 1¾oz balls Gray (shade 3043)
2 × 1¾oz balls Dk. Brown (shade 3011)
1 × 1¾oz balls each of Brown (shade 3009), Med. Brown (3099), Lt. Brown (3098), Dk. Gold (3019), Med. Gold (3012), and Lt. Gold (3006)

Child
5 (5, 6, 6, 7) × 1¾oz balls Gray (shade 3043)
1 × 1¾oz balls each of Med. Brown (shade 3099), Dk. Brown (3011), Brown (3009), Lt. Brown (3098), Dk. Gold (3019), Med. Gold (3012), and Lt. Gold (3006)
Note: apart from the Gray and Med. Brown yarns, the excess yarn from the adult's sweater is sufficient for the child's sweater.
A pair each of sizes 3 and 6 knitting needles
Stitch holder

GAUGE

22 sts. and 30 rows to 4in over pat. worked on size 6 needles

To save time, take time to check gauge.

NOTES

Directions for larger sizes are given in parentheses (). When working motif, use separate, small balls of yarn. When joining in a new color, leave an end of about 2in for weaving in later. When changing color, twist yarns together at back of work to avoid making a hole.

Adult's Sweater

BACK

** Using size 3 needles and gray, cast on 127 sts.
Rib row 1: K.1, * p.1, k.1; rep. from * to end.
Rib row 2: P.1, * k.1, p.1; rep. from * to end.
Rep. these 2 rows for 3in, ending rib row 1.
Inc. row: Rib 6, m.1, * rib 11, m.1; rep. from * to last 11 sts., rib to end: 138 sts.
Change to size 6 needles and work rows 1–100 from Chart A.

"Lionesses" modeled by internationally acclaimed guitarist Mike Rutherford. He was a founder member of Genesis and Mike and the Mechanics. His son Tom models the child's lioness sweater.

LIONESSES

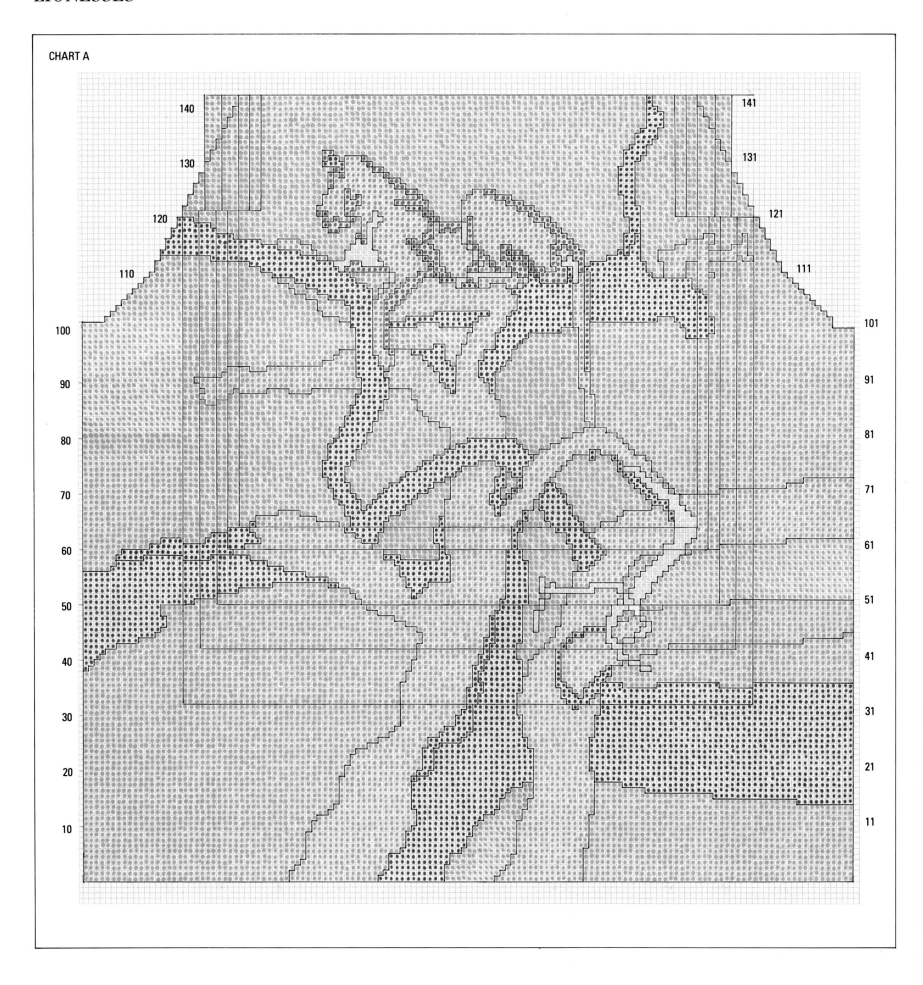

Shape raglans

Working in pat., bind off 4 sts. at beg. of next 2 rows, then dec. 1 st. at each end of foll. 9 rows: 112 sts. **

Now dec. 1 st. at each end of every every alt. row until row 142 from chart has been completed.

Using gray, cont. dec. on every alt. row until 48 sts. rem.

P.1 row.

Shape back neck

Next row: K.2 tog., k.12, turn and leave rem. sts. on a stitch holder.

Next row: Bind off 6 sts., p. to end.

Next row: K.2 tog., k. to end.

Next row: Bind off 5 sts.

Bind off last st.

With RS facing, slip first 20 sts. onto a stitch holder.

Rejoin yarn and k. to last 2 sts., k.2 tog.

P.1 row.

Next row: Bind off 6 sts., k. to last 2 sts., k.2 tog.

P. 1 row.

Bind off.

FRONT

Work as given for back from ** to **, but work from Chart B.

Now dec. 1 st. at each end of every foll. alt. row until row 150 has been completed. Using gray, cont. dec. on every alt. row until 64 sts. rem.

P.1 row.

Shape front neck

Next row: K.2 tog., k.20, turn and leave rem. sts. on a stitch holder.

Work on these sts. only.

Cont. shaping raglan as before, at the same time, dec. 1 st. at neck edge on every row until 4 sts. rem.

Now cont. shaping raglan only, until 1 st. rem.

Bind off.

With RS facing, slip first 20 sts. onto a stitch holder.

Rejoin yarn and k. to last 2 sts., k.2 tog.

Now complete 2nd side of neck to match first side, reversing all shaping.

LEFT SLEEVE

** Using size 3 needles and gray, cast on 61 sts.

Work the 2 rib rows as given for back for 3in, ending rib row 1.

Inc. row: * Rib 6, m.1; rep. from * to last 7 sts., rib to end: 70 sts.

Change to size 6 needles and inc. 1 st. at each end of 5th and every foll. 4th row until there are 78 sts., ending with a p. row. **

Now work rows 1–86 from Chart C, inc. 1 st. at each end of 5th and foll. 6th row until there are 96 sts.

Shape raglans

Keeping pat. correct, bind off 4 sts. at beg. of next 2 rows.

Then dec. 1 st. at each end of next and every foll. alt. row.

When row 106 from chart has been completed, using gray, cont. dec. as before until 10 sts. rem.

Next row: Bind off 5 sts., p. to end.

Bind off.

 (3043)
 (3011)
 (3009)
 (3099)
(3098)
 (3019)
 (3012)
(3006)

LIONESSES

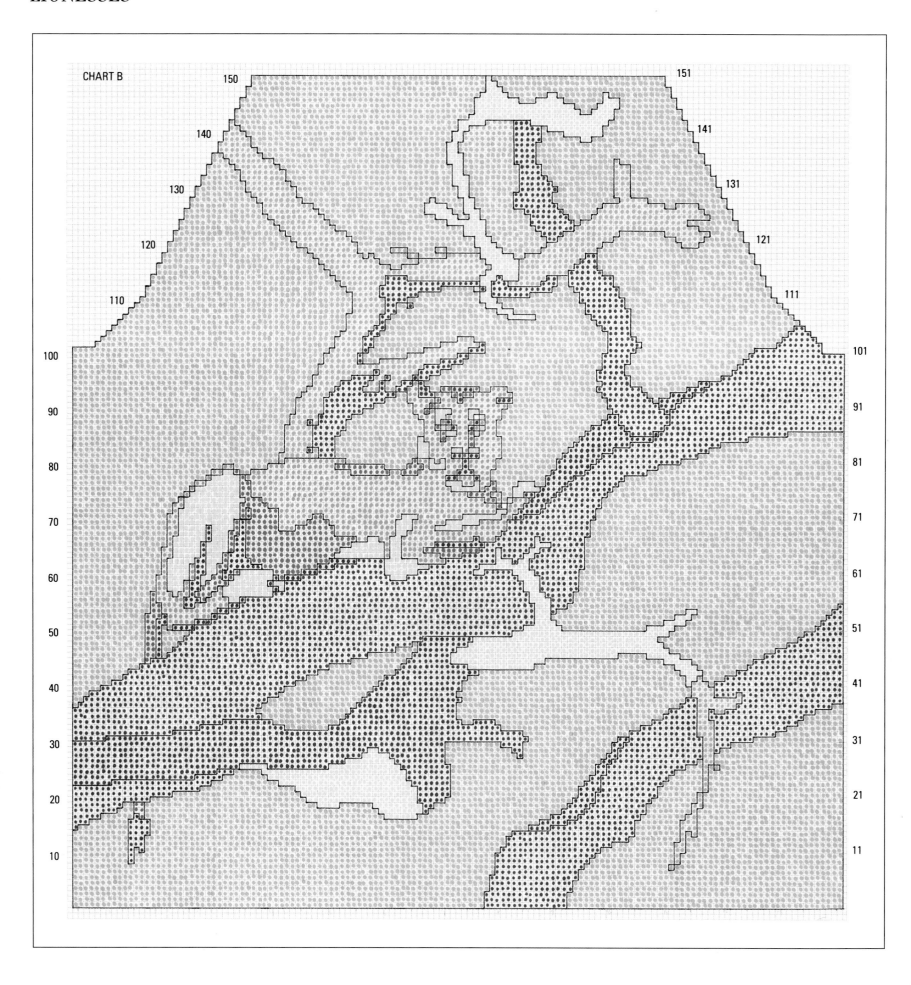

CHART B

RIGHT SLEEVE

Work as given for left sleeve from ** to **.

Now work rows 1–72 from Chart D, inc. 1 st. at each end of 5th and every foll. 6th row until there are 96 sts.

Using gray, work 14 rows even.

Shape raglans

Bind off 4 sts. at beg. of next 2 rows. Then dec. 1 st. at each end of next and every foll. alt. row until 54 sts. rem. Now work rows 1–13 from Chart E.

Using gray, cont. dec. as before until 12 sts. rem.

P. 1 row.

Next row: Bind off 6 sts., k. to last 2 sts., k.2 tog.

P. 1 row.

Bind off rem. 5 sts.

NECKBAND

Join both front and left back raglan seams.

With RS facing, using size 3 needles and gray, pick up and k. 9 sts. down right back neck, k. across 20 sts. from holder, pick up and k. 10 sts. up left back neck, 6 sts. across left sleeve, 16 sts. down left front neck, k. across 20 sts. from holder, pick up and k. 16 sts. up right front neck and k. across 6 sts. from right sleeve: 103 sts.

P. 1 row.

Then work 10 rows rib as given for back.

Bind off in rib.

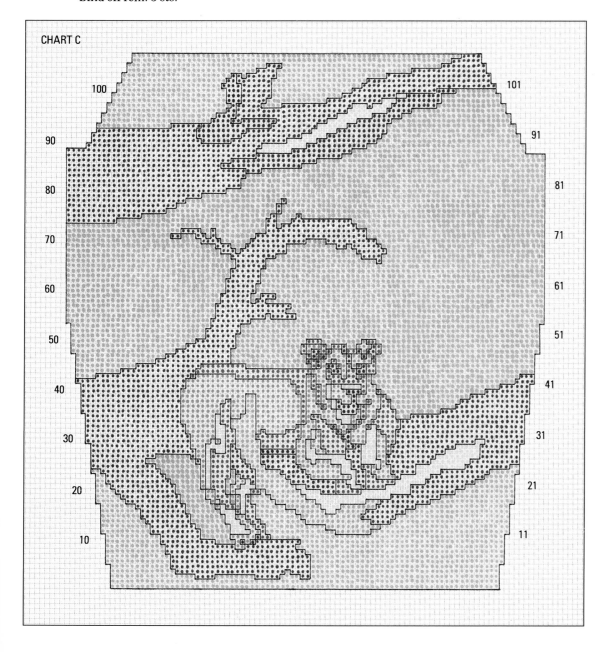

CHART C

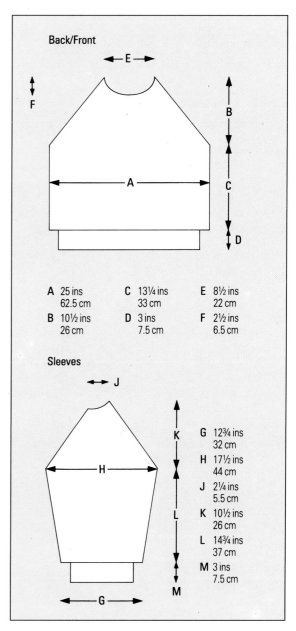

Back/Front

| A | 25 ins 62.5 cm | C | 13¼ ins 33 cm | E | 8½ ins 22 cm |
| B | 10½ ins 26 cm | D | 3 ins 7.5 cm | F | 2½ ins 6.5 cm |

Sleeves

G	12¾ ins 32 cm
H	17½ ins 44 cm
J	2¼ ins 5.5 cm
K	10½ ins 26 cm
L	14¾ ins 37 cm
M	3 ins 7.5 cm

LIONESSES

COLLAR

Using size 3 needles and gray, cast on 103 sts.
Work 32 rows in k.1, p.1 rib as given for back.
Bind off in rib.

TO FINISH

Block and press pieces lightly under a damp cloth foll. yarn label instructions. Join right back raglan to neckband seams. Fold neckband in half to WS and slipstitch in position. Starting at center front, stitch bound-off edge of collar to neckband seam, stitch by stitch. Join side and sleeve seams.

Child's Sweater

BACK

** Using size 3 needles and gray, cast on 77 (81, 85, 91, 97) sts.
Work in rib as given for adult's sweater back for 2½in, ending rib row 1.
Inc. row: Rib 7 (9, 11, 14, 17), m.1, * rib 16, m.1; rep. from * to last 6 (8, 10, 13, 16) sts., rib to end: 82 (86, 90, 96, 102) sts. **
Change to size 6 needles and work 56 (60, 70, 78, 88) rows st.st.

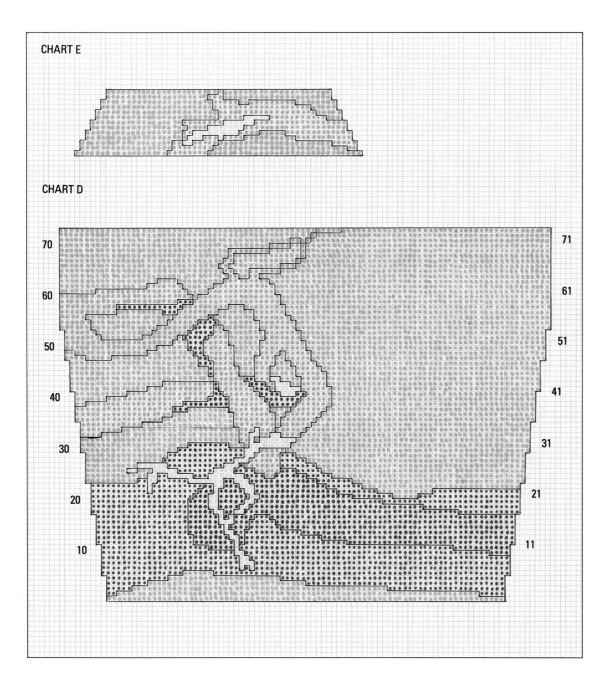

CHART E

CHART D

Shape armholes

Bind off 4 sts. at beg. of next 2 rows: 74 (78, 82, 88, 94) sts.
Work 44 (46, 48, 52, 54) rows even.

Shape back neck

Next row: K.27 (29, 31, 34, 37) sts., turn and leave rem. sts. on a stitch holder.

Work on these sts only.

Next row: Bind off 4 sts., p. to end.

K.1 row.

Next row: Bind off 4(4, 4, 4, 5) sts., p. to end.

Bind off rem. 19 (21, 23, 26, 28) sts.

With RS facing , slip first 20 sts. onto a stitch holder. Rejoin yarn and k. to end.

Complete 2nd side of back neck to match first, reversing all shaping.

FRONT

Work as given for back from ** to **.

Change to size 6 needles and starting at row 65 (61, 51, 43, 33) of Chart A, cont. until row 120 has been completed.

Shape armholes

Bind off 4 sts. at beg. of next 2 rows: 74 (78, 82, 88, 94) sts.
Work until row 142 from chart has been completed.

Using gray, work 12 (14, 16, 18, 18) rows even.

Shape front neck

Next row: K.29 (31, 33, 35, 38) sts., turn and leave rem. sts. on a stitch holder.

Cont. on these sts. only, dec. 1 st. at neck edge only on every row until 19 (21, 23, 25,28) sts. rem.

Work 5 (5, 5, 7, 9) rows even.

Bind off.

With RS facing, slip first 16 (16, 16, 18, 18) sts. onto a stitch holder.

Rejoin yarn and k. to end.

Complete 2nd side of neck to match first side, reversing all shaping.

SLEEVES

Using size 3 needles and gray, cast on 41 (45, 49, 53, 57) sts.

Work in k.1, p.1 rib as given for adult's sweater back for 2½in, ending with rib row 1.

Inc. row: Rib 3 (5, 7, 9, 11), m.1, * rib 6, m.1; rep from * to last 2 (4, 6, 8, 10) sts., rib to end: 48 (52, 56, 60, 64) sts.

Change to size 6 needles and cont. in st.st. inc. 1 st. at each end of 5th and every foll. 6th row until there are 72 (74, 80, 82, 88) sts.

Work even until sleeve measures 14¼ (15, 16, 17¼, 18½)in from beg.

Bind off.

NECKBAND

Join left shoulder seam.

Using size 3 needles and gray, with RS facing, pick up and k.11 (11, 11, 11, 12) sts. down right back neck, k. across 20 sts. from holder, pick up and k.12 (12, 12, 12, 13) sts. up left back neck, 17 (17, 17, 19, 21) sts. down left front neck, k. across 16 (16, 16, 18, 18) sts. from holder, pick up and k.17 (17, 17, 19, 21) sts. up right front neck: 93 (93, 93, 99, 105) sts.

P.1 row.

Rib row 1: K.1 med. gold, * p.1 gray, k.1 med. gold; rep. from * to end.

Rib row 2: P.1 med. gold, * k.1 gray, p.1 med. gold; rep. from * to end.

Rep. these 2 rib rows once more.

Rib row 5: K.1 med. gold, * p.1 dk. brown, k.1 med. gold; rep. from * to end.

Rib row 6: P.1 med. gold, * k.1 dk. brown, p.1 med. gold; rep. from * to end.

Using dk. brown, bind off in rib.

TO FINISH

Block and press pieces lightly under a damp cloth foll. yarn label instructions. Join right shoulder and neckband seam. Joining bound-off edges of armholes to underarms of sleeves, sew in sleeves. Join side and sleeve seams.

Back/Front

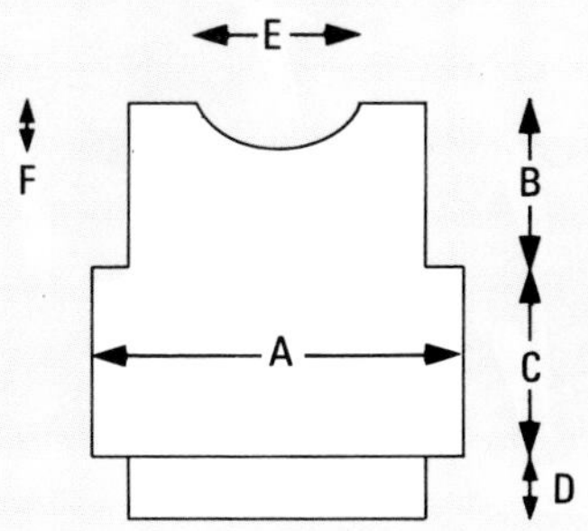

A 14¾ (15½; 16½; 17½; 18½) ins
37 (39; 41; 43.5; 46.5) cm

B 6½ (6¾; 7¼; 7½; 8) ins
16.5 (17; 18; 19; 20) cm

C 7½ (8; 9¼; 10½11½) ins
18.5 (20; 23; 26; 29) cm

D 2½ ins
6 cm

E 6½ (6½; 6½; 6½; 6¾) ins
16.5 (16.5; 16.5; 16.5; 17) cm

F 2 (2; 2; 2½; 2¾) ins
5 (5; 5; 6; 7) cm

Sleeves

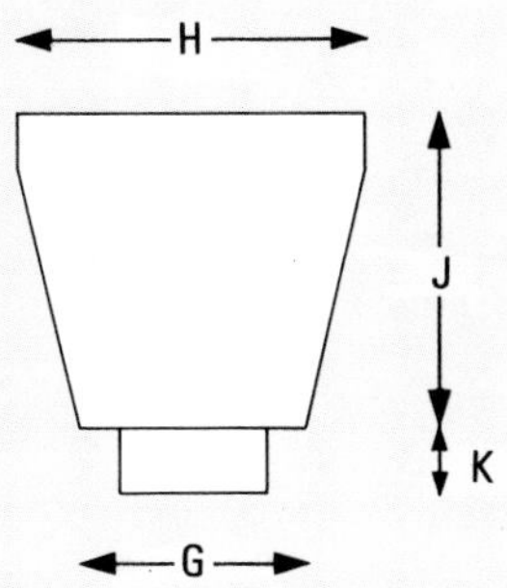

G 8¾ (9½; 10¼; 11; 11½) ins
22 (24; 25.5; 27.5; 29) cm

H 13 (13½; 14½; 15½16) ins
32.5 (34; 36; 37; 40) cm

J 11¾ (12½; 13½; 14¾; 16) ins
29 (31; 34; 37; 40) cm

K 2½ ins
6 cm

The Swans familiar in ornamental parks are Mute Swans. These beautiful birds are residents in northern and central Europe and are still common, although they are subject to many hazards such as poisoning by leadweights used by fishermen, which they accidentally eat, or collision with overhead power cables. More rarely seen are the two smaller species, Bewick's Swan and the Whooping Swan. These breed in the high Arctic tundra and undergo long, hazar-dous migrations to winter in more southern regions, including the British Isles. Although a few are shot on these migrations, they have suffered mainly from the loss of their traditional wetland wintering sites through drainage of the land for conversion to agriculture. Fortunately, several of the remaining wintering sites are now protected in nature reserves, such as that run by the Wildfowl Trust at Slimbridge in south-west England.

Whooper SWANS *and Daffodils*

▶ In strong sunlight, white Swans take on a blue tinge when they stand in shadow. This classic cardigan in soft, gray cotton illustrates this well. Daffodils are added to the sleeves to reflect the yellow on the beaks of these Whooper Swans.

SIZES
To fit 30 (32, 34, 36, 38)in chest.

MATERIALS
Pingouin Corrida 4 (medium-weight cotton)
10 (10, 10, 11, 11) × 1¾oz balls Tourterelle (shade 502)
1 × 1¾oz ball each of Noir (528), Soleil (536), Blanc (501), Myosotis (508), and Vert d'eau (543)
6 × ½in crystal buttons
A pair each of sizes 3 and 6 knitting needles
Stitch holder

GAUGE
20 sts. and 26 rows to 4in over st.st. worked on size 6 needles

To save time, take time to check gauge.

NOTES
Directions for larger sizes are given in parentheses (). When working motifs use separate, small balls of yarn. When joining in a new color, leave an end of about 2in for weaving in later, and when changing color, twist yarns together at back of work to avoid making a hole. If preferred, small areas, such as the grass, may be added later using duplicate stitch, see "Know-How" section.

BACK
Using size 3 needles and tourterelle, cast on 89 (95, 99, 105, 109) sts.
Rib row 1: K.1, * p.1, k.1; rep. from * to end.
Rib row 2: P.1 , * k.1, p.1; rep from * to end.
Rep. 2 rib rows for 1in, inc. 1 st in last row: 90 (96, 100, 106, 110) sts.
Change to size 6 needles and work 36 (40, 40, 42, 46) rows st.st.
Then work rows 1–63 from Chart A.
Work 21 (23, 23, 27, 31) rows st.st.

Shape back neck
Next row: K.35, (38, 40, 43, 45), turn and leave rem. sts. on a stitch stitch holder.
Work on these sts. only
Next row: Bind off 4 sts., p. to end.
K.1 row.
Next row: Bind off 4 (4, 5, 5, 6) sts., p. to end.
Bind off rem. 27 (30, 31, 34, 35) sts.
Return to rem. sts.

"Swans and Daffodils" modeled by actress Elizabeth Hurley, who recently starred in the BBC series Cristobel. *Elizabeth lives in South Kensington and is soon to star in the American mini-series* Act of Will.

SWANS AND DAFFODILS

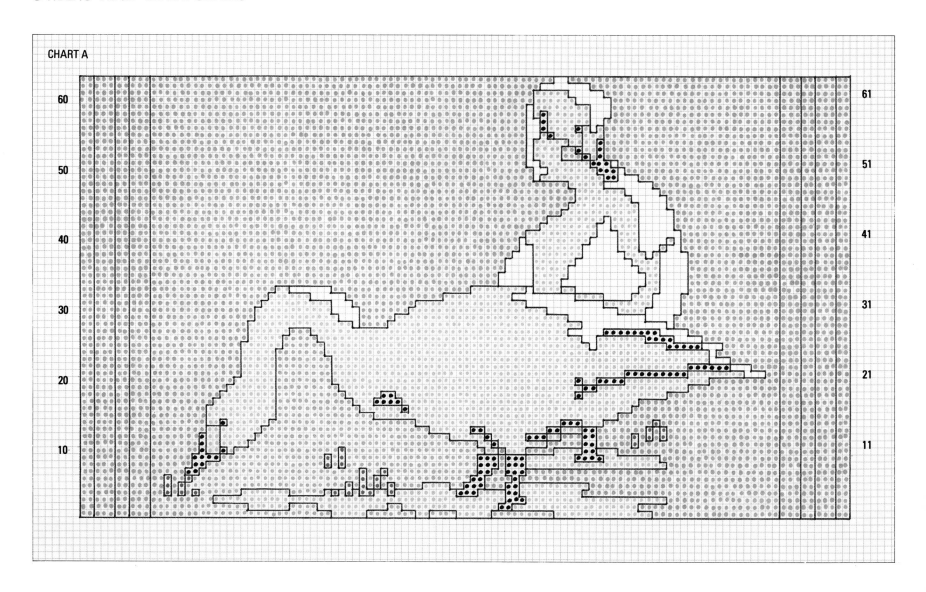

CHART A

Tourterelle (502)

Noir (528)

Soleil (536)

Blanc (501)

Myosotis (508)

Vert D'eau (543)

With RS facing, slip first 20 sts. onto a stitch stitch holder.
Rejoin yarn to first st. and k. to end.
Complete to match first side of back neck, reversing all
shaping.

LEFT FRONT

** Using size 3 needles and tourterelle, cast on 45 (47, 49,
53, 55) sts.
Work 1in in rib as given for back.
For 2nd and 3rd sizes only, inc. 1 st. in last row: 45 (48, 50,
53, 55) sts. **
Change to size 6 needles and work 8 (12, 12, 14, 18) rows
st.st.
Then work rows 1–92 from Chart B.
Work 8 (10, 10, 14, 18) rows st.st.

Shape front neck

Next row: K.35, (38, 40, 43, 45) sts., turn and leave rem.
sts. on a stitch stitch holder.
*** Work on these sts. only, dec 1 st. at neck edge only until
27 (30, 31, 34, 35) sts. rem.
Work 7 (7, 6, 6, 5) rows even.
Bind off. ***

RIGHT FRONT

Work as given for left front from ** to **.
Change to size 6 needles and work 46 (50, 50, 52, 56) rows
st.st.
Work rows 1–35 from Chart C.
Work 28 (30, 30, 34, 38) rows even, ending with a k. row.

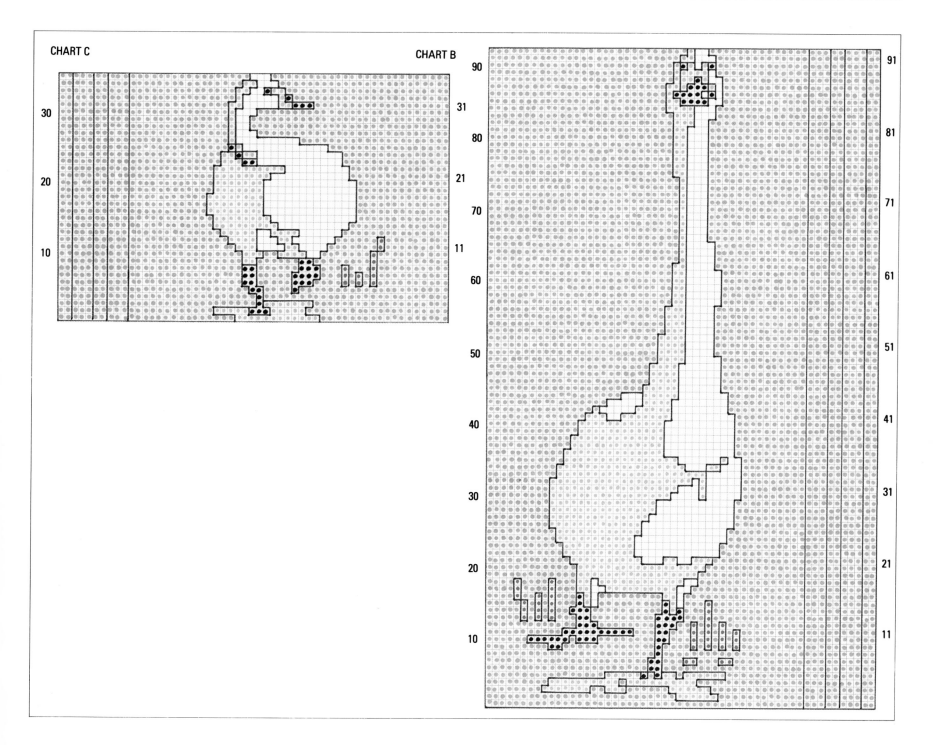

CHART C   **CHART B**

Shape front neck

Next row: P.35 (38, 40, 43, 45) sts., turn and leave rem. sts. on a stitch holder.

Now cont. as given for left front from *** to ***.

SLEEVES

Using size 3 needles and tourterelle, cast on 45 (47, 47, 49, 49) sts.

Work ½in in rib as given for back, inc. 1 st. at end of last row: 46 (48, 48, 50, 50) sts.

Change to size 6 needles and work from row 1 of Chart D, at the same time, inc. 1 st. each end of 5th and every foll. 4th row until there are 86 (90, 90, 92, 92) sts.

Work even until row 88 of chart has been completed.

For 1st, 2nd and 3rd sizes only, work 16 (20, 22) rows even. Bind off.

SWANS AND DAFFODILS

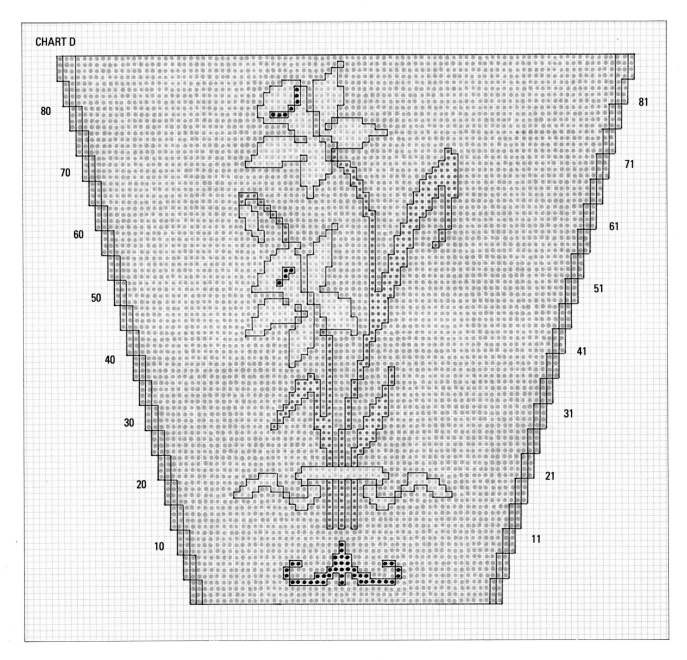

CHART D

80

70

60

50

40

30

20

10

81

71

61

51

41

31

21

11

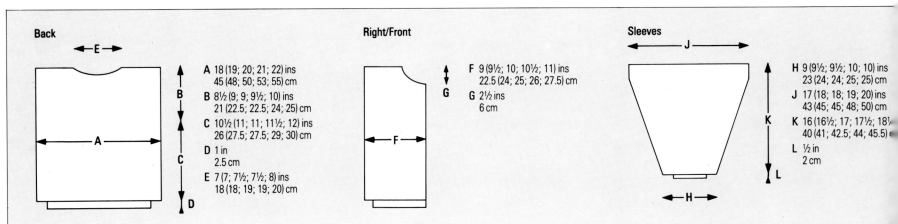

Back

← E →

A 18 (19; 20; 21; 22) ins
   45 (48; 50; 53; 55) cm
B 8½ (9; 9; 9½; 10) ins
   21 (22.5; 22.5; 24; 25) cm
C 10½ (11; 11; 11½; 12) ins
   26 (27.5; 27.5; 29; 30) cm
D 1 in
   2.5 cm
E 7 (7; 7½; 7½; 8) ins
   18 (18; 19; 19; 20) cm

Right/Front

F 9 (9½; 10; 10½; 11) ins
   22.5 (24; 25; 26; 27.5) cm
G 2½ ins
   6 cm

Sleeves

H 9 (9½; 9½; 10; 10) ins
   23 (24; 24; 25; 25) cm
J 17 (18; 18; 19; 20) ins
   43 (45; 45; 48; 50) cm
K 16 (16½; 17; 17½; 18½
   40 (41; 42.5; 44; 45.5)
L ½ in
   2 cm

For 4th and 5th sizes only, cont. inc. as before until there are 96 (100) sts.

Work 21 (17) rows even.

Bind off.

NECK BAND

Join shoulder seams.

Using size 3 needles and tourterelle, with RS facing, starting at right front, k.10 sts. from stitch holder, pick up and k.17 sts. up right front neck, 12 (12, 13, 13, 13) sts. down right back neck, k.20 sts. from stitch holder, pick up and k.13 (13, 14, 14, 14) sts. up left back neck, 17 sts. down left front neck, k.10 sts. from stitch holder: 99 (99, 101, 101, 101) sts.

P.1 row.

Work 4 rows rib as given for back.

Bind off in rib.

BUTTONBAND

Using size 3 needles and tourterelle, with RS facing, pick up and k.91 (97, 97, 101, 107) sts. down left front edge.

Starting rib row 2, work 5 rows rib as given for back.

Bind off in rib.

BUTTONHOLE BAND

Using size 3 needles and tourterelle, with RS facing, pick up and k.91 (97, 97, 101, 107) sts. up right front edge.

Starting rib row 2, rib 1 row as given for back.

Next row: Rib 2 (3, 3, 2, 2), bind off 2 sts., * rib 15 (16, 16, 17, 18), bind off 2 sts.; rep. from * to last 2 (2, 2, 2, 3) sts., rib to end.

Next row: Rib 2 (2, 2, 2, 3), cast on 2 sts. * rib 15 (16, 16, 17, 18), cast on 2 sts.; rep. from * to last 2 (3, 3, 2, 2) sts., rib to end.

Work 2 rows rib.

Bind off in rib.

TO FINISH

Block and press pieces lightly under a damp cloth foll. yarn label instructions. Sew in sleeves. Join side and sleeve seams. Sew on buttons to correspond with buttonholes.

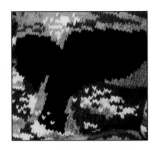

Whales are found in all the major oceans of the world and include the largest animal that has ever lived, the one-hundred-foot long Blue Whale. Mankind has long regarded Whales as valuable sources of oil and meat, and for many years they have been intensively harvested. As a result populations, which once numbered in their hundreds of thousands, have been reduced to a tiny fraction of this.

Increasing concern about the future of Whales reached the point that in 1986 a temporary ban on all large-scale commercial whaling was declared. The rarest and most endangered Whale, the Bowhead, found in the cold northern waters of the Atlantic and Pacific, is still threatened by small-scale hunting carried out by Inuits in the Bering Straits region of Alaska.

ORCAS
Breaching Whales

▶ These bulky oversized sweaters have a definite "marine" feel to them. Bands of jacquard and the phrases "Extinction Is Forever" and "Save The Whale" feature on the back and sleeves. The main motif depicts a "Breaching Whale." A simple cable design completes the effect.

SIZES
Men's sweater (Blue colorway): one size to fit 32–42in chest
Ladies' sweater (Gray colorway): one size to fit 32–42in chest

MATERIALS
Men's Sweater
Pingouin Chunky
9 × 1¾oz balls Marine (shade 15)
4 × 1¾oz balls each of Ecru (shade 10) and Noir (shade 16)
Pingouin Mohican (flecked bulky)
7 × 1¾oz balls Souris (shade 11)
Pingouin Star + (used double)
2 × 1¾oz balls Violet (shade 26)
Ladies' sweater
Pingouin Mohican (flecked bulky)
9 × 1¾oz balls Souris (shade 11)
Pingouin Chunky
6 × 1¾oz balls Ecru (shade 10)
3 × 1¾oz balls each of Noir (shade 16) and Marine (shade 15)

Pingouin Star + (used double)
3 × 1¾oz balls Violet (shade 26)
A pair each of sizes 8 and 10 knitting needles
Stitch holder

GAUGE
13 sts. and 16 rows to 4in over jacquard pat. worked on size 10 needles

To save time, take time to check gauge.

NOTES
When working motif, use separate small balls of yarn. When joining in a new color, leave an end of about 2in for weaving in later and when changing color, twist yarns together at back of work to avoid making a hole.

ABBREVIATIONS
CR2R: cross 2 sts. to the right – K. into front of 2nd st., then k. first st.

Breaching Whale modeled by actor Michael Palin. Ex-Monty Python, Michael Palin has starred in many international motion pictures, such as The Missionary *and* A Fish Called Wanda.

ORCAS

Men's sweater

BACK

** With size 8 needles and marine, cast on 68 sts.

Work cabled rib as follows:

Rib row 1: K.1 , p.2, * k.2, p.2; rep. from * to last st., k.1.

Rib row 2: P.1, k.2, * p.2, k.2; rep. from * to last st., p.1.

Rib row 3: K.1, p.2, * CR2R, p.2; rep. from * to last st., k.1.

Rib row 4: As row 2.

Rep. these 4 rows twice more, then work row 1.

Inc. row: Rib 4, m.1, * rib 5, m.1; rep. from * to last 4 sts, rib to end: 81 sts.

Change to size 10 needles and work rows 5–20 from Chart B **.

Work rows 1–10 of Chart D, placing chart after first 10 sts of souris. Then work rows 1–20 from Chart B, then work Chart E, placing chart after first 33 sts. of souris.

Rep Chart B, then rows 1–10 from Chart F.

Then work rows 1–5 from Chart B.

Next row: Using marine, p.2 tog., p. to end: 80 sts.

*** Using size 10 needles and marine, work 12 rows of cabled rib as at lower edge.

Next row: Bind off 26 sts., k.28, bind off 26 sts.

Leave rem. 28 sts. on a stitch holder.

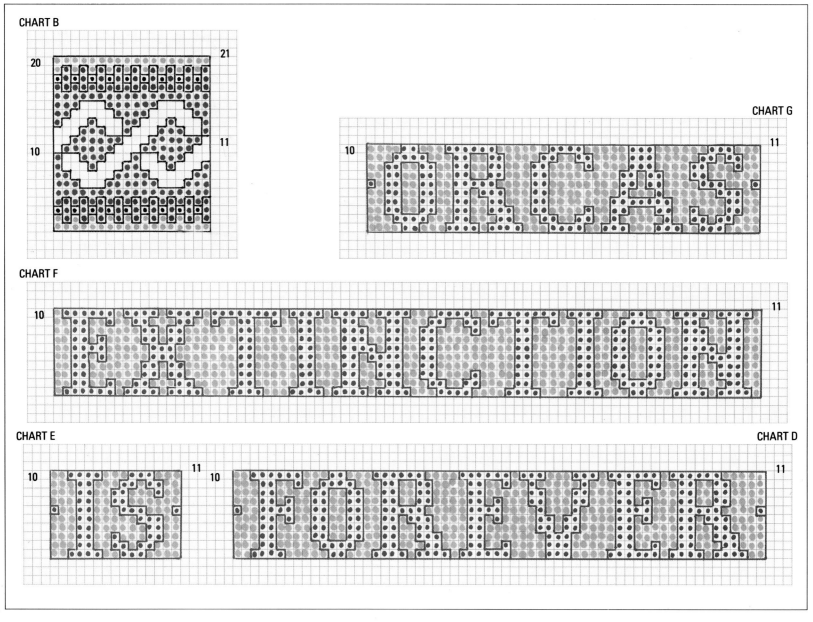

FRONT

Work as given for back from ** to **.

Then work rows 1–53 from Chart A.

Using marine, work 3 rows st.st., then work rows 17–20 from Chart B.

Place Chart G after first 18 sts. of souris.

Work rows 1–5 from Chart B.

Next row: Using marine, p.2 tog., p. to end: 80 sts.

Shape front neck

*** Using size 10 needles, work in cable rib as given for back welt:

Next row: Rib 33 sts, turn and leave rem. sts. on a stitch holder.

Work on these sts. only.

Keeping cable pat. correct, dec. 1 st. at neck edge only on every row until 26 sts. rem.

Work 4 rows even. Bind off in rib.

Return to rem. sts.

With RS facing, slip first 14 sts. onto a stitch holder.

Rejoin yarn and keeping pat. correct, work to end.

Now complete to match first side of neck, reversing all shaping.

CHART A

50 — 40 — 30 — 20 — 10

51 — 41 — 31 — 21 — 11

ORCAS

SLEEVES

Using size 8 needles and marine, cast on 32 sts.

Rep. the 4 cable rib rows as given for back twice, then work row 1.

Inc. row: Rib 1, * m.1, rib 3; rep. from * to last st., rib 1: 43 sts.

Change to size 10 needles and work in pat. from Chart H, working sleeve shaping as indicated until row 74 has been completed: 73 sts.

Bind off.

COLLAR

Join left shoulder seam.

With RS facing, using size 8 needles and marine, k. across 28 sts. of back neck; pick up and k.13 sts. down left front; k. across 14 sts. of front neck; pick up and k.13 sts. up right front: 68 sts.

Rib row 1: K.1, p.2. * k.2, * p.2; rep. from * to last st., k.1.

Rib row 2: P.1, CR2R, * p.2, CR2R; rep. from * to last st., p.1.

Rib row 3: As row 1.

Rib row 4: P.1, k.2, * p.2, k.2; rep. from * to last st., p.1.

Rep 4 cable rib rows twice more.

Bind off in rib.

TO FINISH

Block and press pieces lightly under a damp cloth foll. yarn label instructions. Join right shoulder and collar seams. Sew in sleeves. Then join side and sleeve seams.

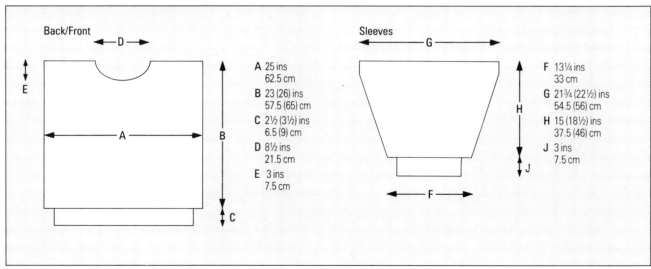

Back/Front

Sleeves

A 25 ins
62.5 cm

B 23 (26) ins
57.5 (65) cm

C 2½ (3½) ins
6.5 (9) cm

D 8½ ins
21.5 cm

E 3 ins
7.5 cm

F 13¼ ins
33 cm

G 21¾ (22½) ins
54.5 (56) cm

H 15 (18½) ins
37.5 (46) cm

J 3 ins
7.5 cm

CHART H

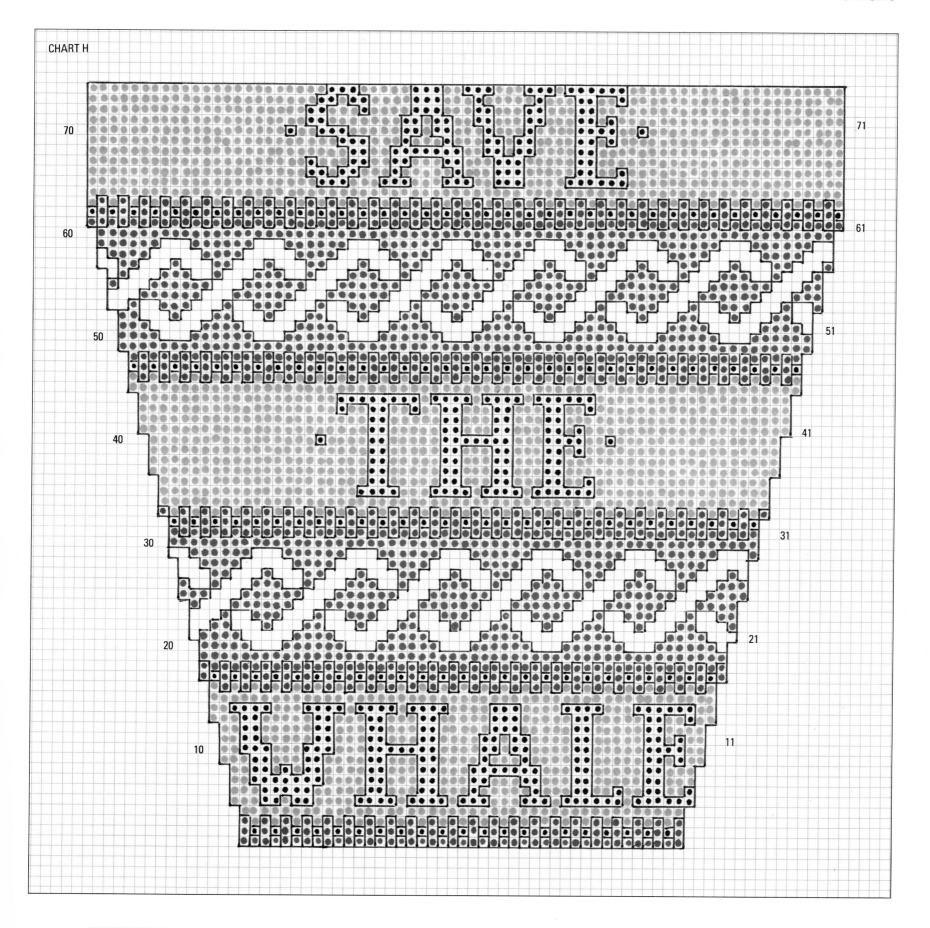

"Breaching Whale" modeled by Susan George, who has starred in over thirty motion pictures, most notably Peckinpah's Straw Dogs. She is currently producing films with her company, Amy International Productions.

Ladies' sweater

Note: Follow 2nd Colorway to work Charts B, D, E, F, G and H.

BACK

** Using size 8 needles and souris, cast on 68 sts.
Rep. the 4 rib rows as given for men's back, twice.
Then work rib row 1. Work inc. row as before: 81 sts.
Change to size 10 needles.
Work rows 17–20 from Chart B.**
Then position Charts D and E side by side as follows:
Row 1: K.1 ecru, k. row 1 from Chart D, k.3 ecru, k. row 1 from Chart E, k.1 ecru.
When these 10 rows have been completed, * work from Chart B, then Chart C; rep from * once more.
Then work rows 1–5 from Chart B.
Next row: Using souris, p.2 tog., p. to end: 80 sts.
Complete in souris as for men's back from *** to end.

FRONT

Work as given for ladies' back from ** to **.
Work Chart F, then work rows 1–4 from Chart B.

Work rows 1–53 from Chart A, then 2 rows st.st. using marine.
Next row: P.1 marine * p.1 noir, p.1 marine; rep. from * to end.
Work rows 3–5 from Chart B.
Using souris, work 1 row st.st., dec. 1 st. at beg. of row: 80 sts.
Now complete as given for men's front from *** to end, using souris.

SLEEVES

Using size 8 needles and souris, cast on 32 sts.
Work cuffs and rows 1–34 from Chart H as given for men's sleeves: 43 sts.
Now set chart C as follows:
Row 1: K.5 ecru, * k.1 violet, k.5 ecru; rep. from * to end.
Cont. shaping sleeves as before and complete Chart C.
Then work rows 45–60 from Chart H: 71 sts.
Bind off.

COLLAR

Using souris, work collar as given for men's collar.

TO FINISH

As given for men's sweater.

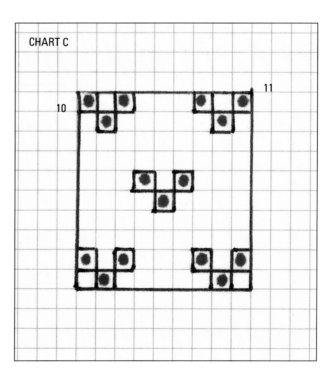

CHART C

Soaring over mountains and forests, the Golden Eagle is without doubt one of the most majestic of all birds. It is also one of the most widespread, being found through much of the northern hemisphere, particularly in temperate regions of North America, Europe, and Asia. Unfortunately, wherever Golden Eagles are found they come into conflict with farmers who accuse them of preying on newborn lambs. As a consequence they have been poisoned and trapped, and even shot from airplanes, in large numbers. They have also, like all birds of prey, suffered from the excessive use of pesticides which build up in the food they eat and can cause them to lay infertile or thin-shelled and easily broken eggs. Improved environmental controls have decreased this problem to some extent in recent years. This, and the legal protection now given to Golden Eagles in many countries, has allowed some populations to start recovering slowly.

Golden EAGLE

▶ This tunic-style sweater is emblazoned with stitchery, beading and embroidery. The design focuses on the intense and sharp-sighted eyes of this magnificent bird of prey – its right wing unfolding, it is aware of danger. The Celtic patterning complements the Eagle's coloring.

SIZES
To fit 32 (34, 36, 38)in chest.

MATERIALS
Emu Superwash medium-weight 100% wool
9 (9, 10, 10) × 1¾oz balls Dk. Gray (shade 3071)
2 × 1¾oz balls each of Black (shade 3070), Dk. Gold (3019)
1 × 1¾oz ball each of Green (shade 3075), Purple (3052), Lt. Gray (3080), Brown (3009), White (3078), Lt. Gold (3006), and Dk. Brown (3011)
A pair each of sizes 3 and 6 knitting needles
Small beads
Stitch holder

GAUGE
23 sts. and 27 rows to 4in over st.st. pat. worked on size 6 needles
To save time, take time to check gauge.

ABBREVIATIONS
CR2R: cross 2 sts. to the right – K. into front of 2nd st., then k. first st.
CR2L: cross 2 sts. to the left – K. into back of 2nd st., then k. first st.
Sl.1 – Slip 1 st. purlwise.

FEATHER STITCH (Over 18 sts.)
Row 1: * K.8, p. 1; rep. from * to end.
Row 2: * K.1, p.8; rep. from * to end.
Row 3: * K.8, p.3, CR2R, CR2L, p.3; rep. from * to end.
Row 4: * K.3, sl.1, p.2, sl.1, k.3, p.8; rep. from * to end.
Row 5: * K.8, p.2,CR2R, k.2, CR2L, p.2; rep. from * to end.
Row 6: * K.2, sl.1, p.4, sl.1, k.2, p.8; rep. from * to end.
Row 7: * K.8, p.1, CR2R, k.4, CR2L, p.1; rep. from * to end.
Row 8: * K.1, sl.1, p.6, sl.1, k.1, p.8; rep. from * to end.
Row 9: As row 1.
Row 10: As row 2.
Row 11: * P.2, CR2R, CR2L, p.3, k.8, p.1; rep. from * to end.
Row 12: K.1, p.8, k.3, sl.1, p.2, sl.1, k.2; rep. from * to end.
Row 13: * P.1, CR2R, k.2, CR2L, p.2, k.8, p.1; rep. from * to end.
Row 14: * K.1, p.8, k.2, sl.1, p.4, sl.1, k.1; rep. from *to end.
Row 15: * CR2R, k.4, CR2L, p.1, k.8, p.1; rep. from * to end.
Row 16: * K.1, p.8, k.1, sl.1, p.6, sl.1; rep. from * to end.
These 16 rows form pat.

"Golden Eagle" modeled by multi-lingual actress Rula Lenska, who has appeared in countless TV and theatre productions. Rula is passionate about conservation and dedicates a lot of her spare time to the WWF. She is also the narrator on Anglia TVs production Survival.

GOLDEN EAGLE

- ⬤ (3071)
- ⬤ (3070)
- ⬤ (3019)
- ⬤ (3011)
- ☐ (3078)
- ⬤ (3080)
- ⬤ (3052)
- ⬤ (3075)
- ⬤ (3009)
- ⬤ (3006)
- ☒ Cross stitch using black (3070)

NOTES

Directions for the larger sizes are given in parentheses ().
When working motif, use separate, small balls of yarn.
When joining in a new color, leave an end of about 2in for weaving in later, and when changing color, twist yarns together at back of work to avoid making a hole.

BACK

** Using size 3 needles and black, cast on 103 (109, 115, 121) sts.

Rib row 1: K.1 dk. gray, * p.1 black, k.1 dk. gray; rep. from * to end.

Rib row 2: P.1 dk. gray, * k.1 black, p.1 dk. gray; rep. from * to end.

Rep. these 2 rows once more, inc. 1 st. at end of last row: 104 (110, 116, 122) sts.

Change to size 6 needles and work rows 1–58 from Chart A. **

Row 59: Work row 1 of feather st., placing pat. by working K.2 (5, 8, 2), p.1, * k.8, p.1; rep. from * to last 2 (5, 8, 2) sts., k. to end.

Row 60: Keeping pat. correct, work from row 2 of feather pat.

Cont. in feather st. until 4 complete reps. have been worked, then work rows 1–8 once more.

Shape armholes

Bind off 4 sts. at beg. of next 2 rows. Cont. working feather st. pat. on rem. 96 (102, 108, 114) sts. until 6 complete pat. reps. have been worked, then work rows 1 and 2 once more.

Work rows 1–46 (46, 48, 52) from Chart C.

Shape back neck

Next row: K.36 (38, 40, 42), turn and leave rem. sts. on a stitch holder.

Work on these sts. only.

Next row: Bind off 5 sts., p. to end.

K.1 row.

Next row: Bind off 6 sts., p. to end.

Bind off. Return to rem. sts.

With RS facing, slip first 24 (26, 28, 30) sts. onto a stitch holder.

Rejoin yarn to first st. and k. to end.

Complete 2nd side of back neck to match first side, reversing all shaping.

FRONT

Work as given for back from ** to **.

Work 2 rows in dk. gray.

Work rows 1–96 from Chart B, shaping armholes at beg. of rows 71 and 72: 96 (102, 108, 114) sts.

Now work rows 1–28 (28, 30, 34) from Chart C.

Shape front neck

Next row: Working in pat., k.38 (41, 44, 47), turn and leave rem. sts. on a spare needle.

Work on these sts. only.

Dec. 1 st. at neck edge only until 25 (27, 29, 31) sts. rem.

Work 8 (7, 6, 5) rows even.

Bind off.

Return to rem. sts.

With RS facing, slip first 20 sts. onto a stitch holder.

Rejoin yarn to first st., k. to end.

Complete 2nd side of front neck to match first side, reversing all shaping.

CHART C

CHART A

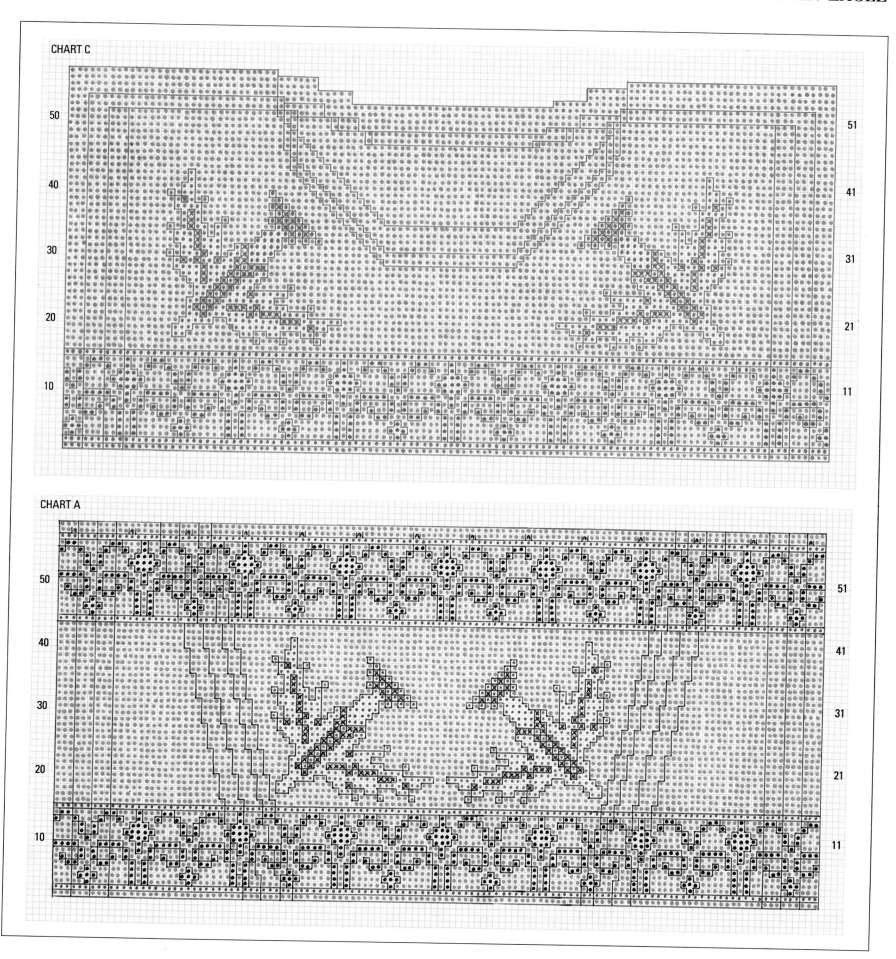

GOLDEN EAGLE

CHART B

SLEEVES

Using size 3 needles and black, cast on 45 (49, 55, 61) sts.
Rep. 2 rib rows as given for back twice, inc. 1 st. at end of
last row: 46 (50, 56, 62) sts.
Change to size 6 needles and work from row 1 of Chart A,
shaping sleeve by inc. 1 st. each end of 5th and every foll.
4th row until there are 74 (78, 84, 90) sts.

Change to dk. gray.

Row 59: Work row 1 of feather st. placing pat. by working
k.5 (7, 1, 4), p.1, * k.8, p.1; rep. from * to last 5 (7, 1, 4) sts.,
k. to end.

Row 60: Keeping pat. correct, work row 2 of feather st. pat.
Cont. from row 3 of feather st. pat. and at same time, inc. 1
st. each end of next and every foll. 4th row until there are

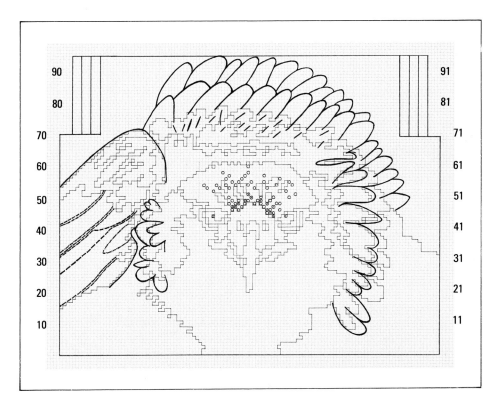

110 (110, 116, 122) sts., taking all inc. sts. into feather st. pat.

Work 11 (19, 19, 19) rows even.

Bind off.

COLLAR

Join left shoulder seam.

Using size 3 needles and dk. gray, pick up and k.9 sts. down right back neck, k. across 24 (26, 28, 30) sts. from holder, pick up and k.10 sts. up left back neck, pick up and k.21 sts. down left front neck, k. across 20 sts. from holder, pick up and k.21 sts. up right front neck: 105 (107, 109, 111) sts.

Rib row 1: Using dk. gray, p.1, * k.1, p.1; rep. from * to end.

Rib row 2: K.1 black, * p.1 dk. gray, k.1 black; rep. from * to end.

Rib row 3: P.1 black, * k.1 dk. gray, p.1 black; rep. from * to end.

Rib row 4: K.1 black, * p.1 purple, k.1 black; rep. from * to end.

Rib row 5: P.1 black, * k.1 purple, p.1 black; rep. from * to end.

Rep rows 4 and 5, 4 times more.

Using black, bind off.

TO FINISH

Block and press pieces lightly under a damp cloth foll. yarn label instructions. Join right shoulder and collar seam. Work backstitch embroidery and French knots as shown on Chart B. Using black, work thistles in duplicate stitch as indicated on Charts A and C. Joining bound-off edge of armholes to underarms of sleeves, sew in sleeves, then join side and sleeve seams. Sew on pairs of beads at points of feather stitch on back and sleeves.

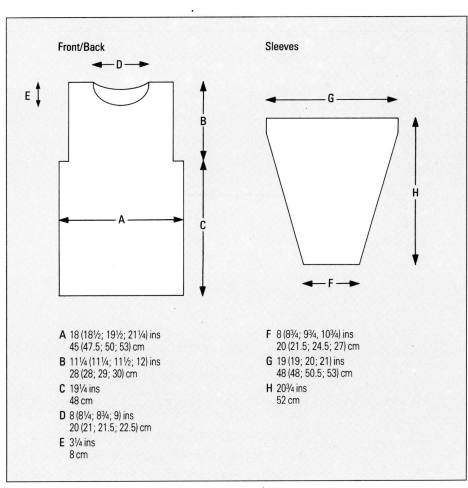

Front/Back   **Sleeves**

A 18 (18½; 19½; 21¼) ins
45 (47.5; 50; 53) cm

B 11¼ (11¼; 11½; 12) ins
28 (28; 29; 30) cm

C 19¼ ins
48 cm

D 8 (8¼; 8¾; 9) ins
20 (21; 21.5; 22.5) cm

E 3¼ ins
8 cm

F 8 (8¾; 9¾; 10¾) ins
20 (21.5; 24.5; 27) cm

G 19 (19; 20; 21) ins
48 (48; 50.5; 53) cm

H 20¾ ins
52 cm

▨ Backstitch embroidery using Black (3070)	⊡ French Knot using Black (3070)
▧ Backstitch embroidery using White (3078)	◉ French Knot using Lt. Gray (3080)
▨ Backstitch embroidery using Lt. Gold (3006)	

Running for 1,200 miles off the coast of Queensland in eastern Australia, the Great Barrier Reef is the world's largest coral reef and one of the most colorful places on earth. Like all such reefs it is made up of the stony skeletons of millions of tiny coral polyps. The coral colonies grow in an extraordinary variety of shapes to produce fantastic underwater landscapes which support myriad other forms of life, including fish, lobsters, starfish, and sea-shells of all description. Coral reefs are only found in shallow tropical sea water and are threatened everywhere by mining for sand and coral rock for building, pollution, and destructive fishing methods including dynamiting and poisoning. Fortunately, most of the Great Barrier Reef is included in a national park where man's activities are carefully controlled and visitors can enjoy the reef's unparalleled beauties without destroying them.

Great
BARRIER REEF

▶ The exotic shape of this little dress is the perfect choice for this tropical theme. The soft cotton yarn and stitchery provide the wealth of color and texture needed to portray the riches of the coral reef.

SIZES
To fit 32 (34, 36)in chest.

MATERIALS
Pingouin Corrida 4 (medium-weight cotton)
8 (8, 9) × 1¾oz balls Noir (shade 528)
1 × 1¾oz ball each of Tourterelle (502), Soleil (536), Corail (542), Lagon (517), Feu (514), Myosotis (508), and Vert d'eau (543)
A pair each of sizes 3 and 6 knitting needles
One size 3 circular knitting needle
Stitch holder

GAUGE
20 sts. and 26 rows to 4in over pat. worked on size 6 needles

To save time, take time to check gauge.

NOTES
Directions for larger sizes are given in parentheses ().
When working motifs use separate, small balls of yarn.
When joining in a new color, leave an end of about 2in for weaving in later. When changing color, twist yarns together at back of work to avoid making a hole.

ABBREVIATIONS
See key on diagram
Nobble – (K.1, k.1 tbl, k.1) all in same stitch, turn, p.3, turn, k.3 tog.
CR2R – K. into front of 2nd st., then k. first st.
CR2L – K. into back of 2nd st., then k. first st.

BACK
** Using size 3 needles and noir, cast on 83 (89, 95) sts.
Rib row 1: K.1, * p.1, k.1; rep from * to end.
Rib row 2: P.1, * k.1, p.1; rep. from * to end.
Rep. 2 rib rows twice more, then row 1 once more.
Change to size 6 needles.
Dec. row: P.5 (3, 7), p.2 tog., * p.5 (6, 6), p.2 tog.; rep from * to last 6 (4, 6) sts., p. to end: 72 (78, 84) sts.
Work 10 rows st.st.
Work from row 1 of Chart A, shaping sides as indicated on chart, ** until row 160 has been completed: 70 (74, 78) sts.

Shape back neck

Next row: Work 25 (27, 29) sts. in pat., turn and leave rem. sts. on a stitch holder.

Work on these sts. only.

Next row: Bind off 3 sts., pat. to end.

Keeping pat. correct, bind off 2 sts. at beg. of foll. 4 alt. rows. Then dec. 1 st. at beg. of foll. 6 (7, 8) alt. rows: 8 (9, 10) sts.

Work 8 rows even.

*** *Next row:* Bind off 4 (5, 5) sts., k. to end.

P.1 row. Bind off rem. 4 (4, 5) sts.

With RS facing, slip first 20 sts. onto a stitch holder ***.

Rejoin yarn to first st. and k. to end.

Complete 2nd side of back neck to match first side, reversing all shaping.

FRONT

Work as given for back from ** to **, then cont. from chart until row 148 has been completed: 72 (76, 80) sts.

Shape front neck

Next row: K.2, k.2 tog., k.22 (24, 26) sts., turn and leave rem sts. on a stitch holder.

Work on these sts. only.

Next row: Bind off 4 sts., p. to end.

Bind off 3 sts. at beg. of next alt. row.

Then, keeping pat. correct, bind off 2 sts. at beg. of foll. 3 alt. rows, then dec. 1 st. at beg. of foll. 4 (5, 6) alt. rows: 8 (9, 10) sts.

Work 24 rows even, then work as given for back from *** to ***.

Rejoin yarn to first st. and k. to last 4 sts., k.2 tog. tbl, k.2.

Complete 2nd side of front neck to match first side, reversing all shaping.

RIGHT SLEEVE

** Using size 3 needles and noir, cast on 57 (61, 65) sts.

Work 5 rows rib as given for back.

Change to size 6 needles.

Dec. row: P.6 (6, 4), p.2 tog., * p.5 (6, 7), p.2 tog.; rep. from * to last 7 (5, 5) sts., p. to end **: 50 (54, 58) sts.

"Great Barrier Reef"
modeled by Marie Helvin.

GREAT BARRIER REEF

CHART A

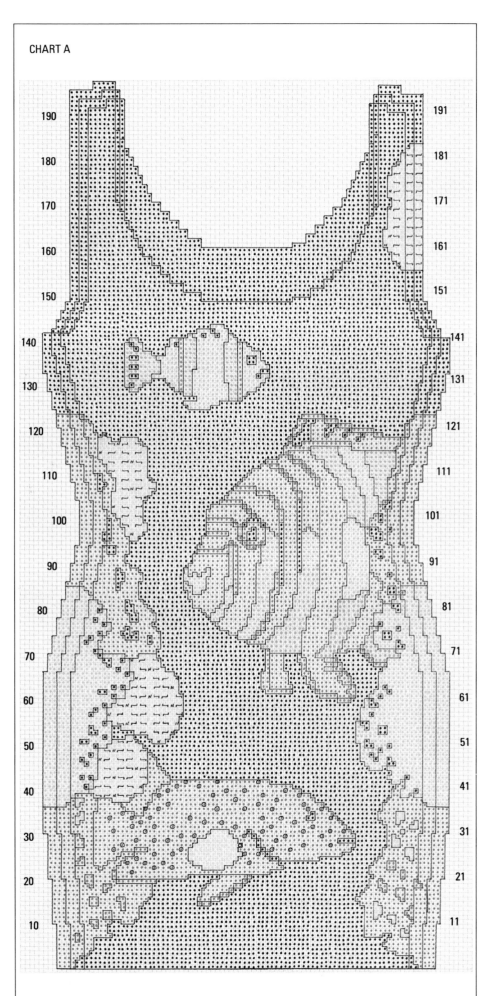

●	Noir (528)
●	Tourterelle (502)
●	Soleil (536)
●	Feu (514)
●	Myosotis (508)
□	Corail (542)
●	Vert D'eau (543)
●	Lagon (517)
⌐	CR2R
⌐	CR2L
N	Nobble using Coral (542)
◎	Half french-knot using Lagon (517)

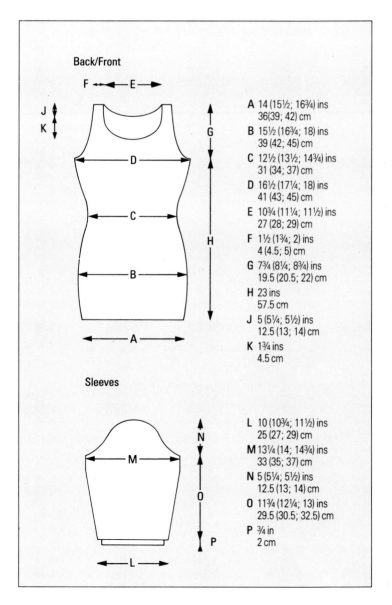

Back/Front

A 14 (15½; 16¾) ins
36 (39; 42) cm

B 15½ (16¾; 18) ins
39 (42; 45) cm

C 12½ (13½; 14¾) ins
31 (34; 37) cm

D 16½ (17¼; 18) ins
41 (43; 45) cm

E 10¾ (11¼; 11½) ins
27 (28; 29) cm

F 1½ (1¾; 2) ins
4 (4.5; 5) cm

G 7¾ (8¼; 8¾) ins
19.5 (20.5; 22) cm

H 23 ins
57.5 cm

J 5 (5¼; 5½) ins
12.5 (13; 14) cm

K 1¾ ins
4.5 cm

Sleeves

L 10 (10¾; 11½) ins
25 (27; 29) cm

M 13¼ (14; 14¾) ins
33 (35; 37) cm

N 5 (5¼; 5½) ins
12.5 (13; 14) cm

O 11¾ (12¼; 13) ins
29.5 (30.5; 32.5) cm

P ¾ in
2 cm

Cont. in st.st. inc. 1 st. at each end of 5th and every foll. 8th row until there are 62 (66, 72) sts.

Work 1 (5, 1) rows. Then work rows 55–84 from Chart B.

Shape cap

*** Bind off 2 sts. at beg. of next 4 rows. Then keeping pat. correct, dec 1 st. at beg. of every row until 40 (44, 48) sts. rem.

Then bind off 2 sts. at beg. of next 6 (8, 10) rows and 3 sts. at beg. of foll. 4 rows.

Bind off rem. 16 sts. ***

LEFT SLEEVE

Work as given for right sleeve from ** to **.

Work from row 9 (5, 1) to row 51 of Chart B, at the same time, shape sleeve by inc. 1 st. each end of 5th and every foll. 8th row until there are 66 (70, 74) sts.

Work 15 (19, 23) rows even.

Cont. as given for right sleeve from *** to ***.

NECKBAND

Join left shoulder seam.

Using size 3 circular knitting needle and noir, with RS facing, pick up and k.39 (40, 41) sts. down right back neck, k.20 sts. from holder, pick up and k.40 (41, 42) sts. up left back neck, 47 (48, 49) sts. down left front neck, k.20 sts. from holder, pick up and k.47 (48, 49) sts. up right front neck: 213 (217, 221) sts.

Starting rib row 2, work 3 rows rib as given for back.

Bind off in rib.

TO FINISH

Block and press pieces lightly under a damp cloth foll. yarn label instructions. Join right shoulder and neckband seams. Join side seams. Join sleeve seams. Pin sleeves into armholes matching pattern. Sew in sleeves. Using lagon, work 'Half French knot' embroidery on lower fish as indicated on chart.

Key to chart

N – Nobble

CR2R   See abbreviations

CR2L

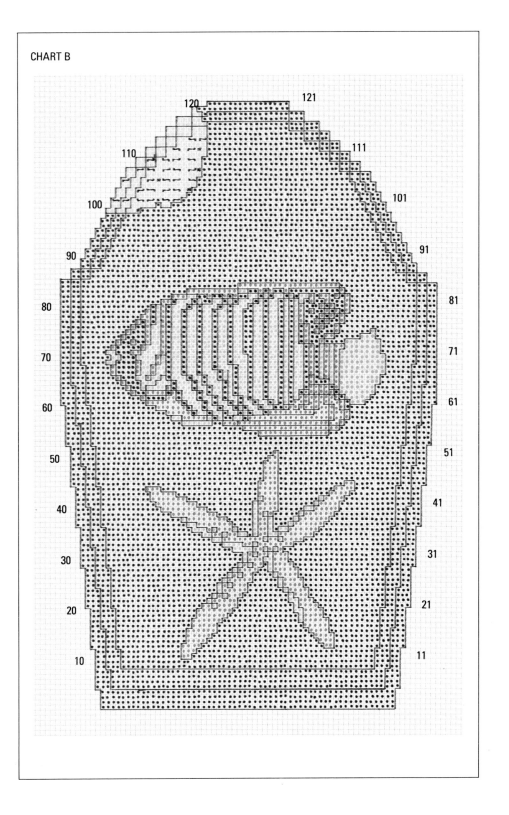

CHART B

Tallest of all land animals, Giraffes stalk the tropical savannahs and woodlands of Africa. Their great height not only allows them to browse in the tops of trees, but also helps them spot potential predators from a distance. While this helps protect them from wild animals such as lions, it is less useful against man, and Giraffes have proved easy targets for hunters. They have been killed for food, for sport, *and for their skins and tails which are used to make fly-swatches. In western Africa, such killing and the loss of their habitat to agriculture and livestock raising has meant that Giraffes have become very rare. In East Africa, how-ever, they are still common, particularly in national parks and game reserves such as the Serengeti National Park in Tanzania and the Amboseli Game Reserve in Kenya.*

GIRAFFES
Browsing in the Savannah

▶ "Tarzan meets Calamity Jane". This safari suit has Western-style fringe and knitted patch pockets. The fringe represents the Giraffe's mane and the ribbed yoke gives the jacket a quilted look.

SIZES
Jacket
One size to fit 32–38in bust.
Skirt
To fit 34 (36, 38)in hips, in two lengths.

MATERIALS
Pingouin France + (used double)
Jacket
13 × 50g balls Ocre (shade 29)
4 × 50g balls Ecru (shade 17)
1 × 50g ball Noir (shade 29)
2½yd × 3in fringe
5 × ¾in and 2 × ⅝in brass buttons
Skirt
Mini version
4 (4, 5) × 50g balls Ocre (shade 29)
1 (1, 2) × 50g balls Ecru (shade 17)
Add one ball of each shade for longer length
⅞yd or 1⅛yd × 3in fringe
6in zipper to match skirt
A pair each of sizes 6 and 7 knitting needles
Stitch holder

GAUGE
16 sts. and 22 rows to 4in over pat. worked on size 7 needles

To save time, take time to check gauge.

NOTES
Directions for larger sizes are given in parentheses (). When working pattern, use separate, small balls of yarn. When joining in a new color, leave an end of about 2in for weaving in later. When changing color, twist yarns together to avoid making a hole.

BACK
Using size 6 needles and ocre, cast on 75 sts.
Rib row 1: K.1, * p.1, k.1; rep. from * to end.
Rib row 2: P.1, * k.1, p.1; rep. from * to end.
Rep. these 2 rows for 15 rows, ending rib row 1.
Inc. row: Rib 8, m.1, * rib 6, m.1; rep. from * to last 7 sts., rib to end: 86 sts.
Change to size 7 needles and work from row 17 of chart, setting pat. as follows:
Row 17: K.25 ocre, k.3 ecru, k.16 ocre, k.4 ecru, k.16 ocre, k.5 ecru, k.11 ocre, k.6 ecru.

"Giraffe" modeled by Mandy Smith. As a model Mandy graced the front covers of countless magazines. She now has a string of hit singles to her credit.

GIRAFFE

Cont. working from chart, shaping armholes by binding off 4 sts. at beg. of rows 77 and 78: 78 sts.

When row 86 of chart has been completed, using ocre work 2 rows dec. 1 st. at beg. of 2nd row: 77 sts.

Rib row 1: K.1, * p.1, k.1; rep. from * to end.

Rib row 2: P.1, k.1, * yo, sl.1 purlwise, k.1; rep. from * to last st., p.1.

Rib row 3: K.1 , p.1, * k.1 tog. with sl.st., p.1; rep. from * to last st., k.1. Rep. rib rows 2 and 3 until 41 rows of rib have been worked, ending rib row 3.

Shape back neck

Working in rib as set, rib 29 sts., turn and leave rem. sts. on a stitch holder.

Next row: Bind off 5 sts., rib to end: 24 sts.

Rib 1 row. Bind off in rib.

Return to sts. on stitch holder, with WS facing, slip first 19 sts. onto stitch holder.

Rejoin yarn to rem. sts. and rib to end. Complete 2nd side of back neck to match first side, reversing all shaping.

LEFT FRONT

Using size 6 needles and ocre, cast on 43 sts.

Work 15 rows rib as given for back, ending rib row 1.

Inc. row: Rib 13, m.1, * rib 4, m.1; rep from * to last 6 sts., rib 6: 50 sts.

Change to size 7 needles and work from row 17 of chart placing pat. as follows:

Row 17: K.25 ocre, k.3 ecru, k.15 ocre, turn and leave rem. 7 sts. on a stitch holder.

Work on these 43 sts. only from row 18 to row 76 of chart.

Shape armhole

Bind off 4 sts. at beg. of row 77: 39 sts.

** When row 86 of chart has been completed, using ocre work 2 rows.

Now work 3 rib rows as given for jacket back yoke, then rep. rows 2 and 3 ** until 28 rib rows have been completed, ending rib row 2.

*** *Next row:* Rib in pat. to last 7 sts., turn and leave rem. sts. on a stitch holder.

Work on these sts. only.

Dec. 1 st. at neck edge only on every row until 24 sts. rem. Work 7 rows even.

Bind off in rib. ***

GIRAFFE

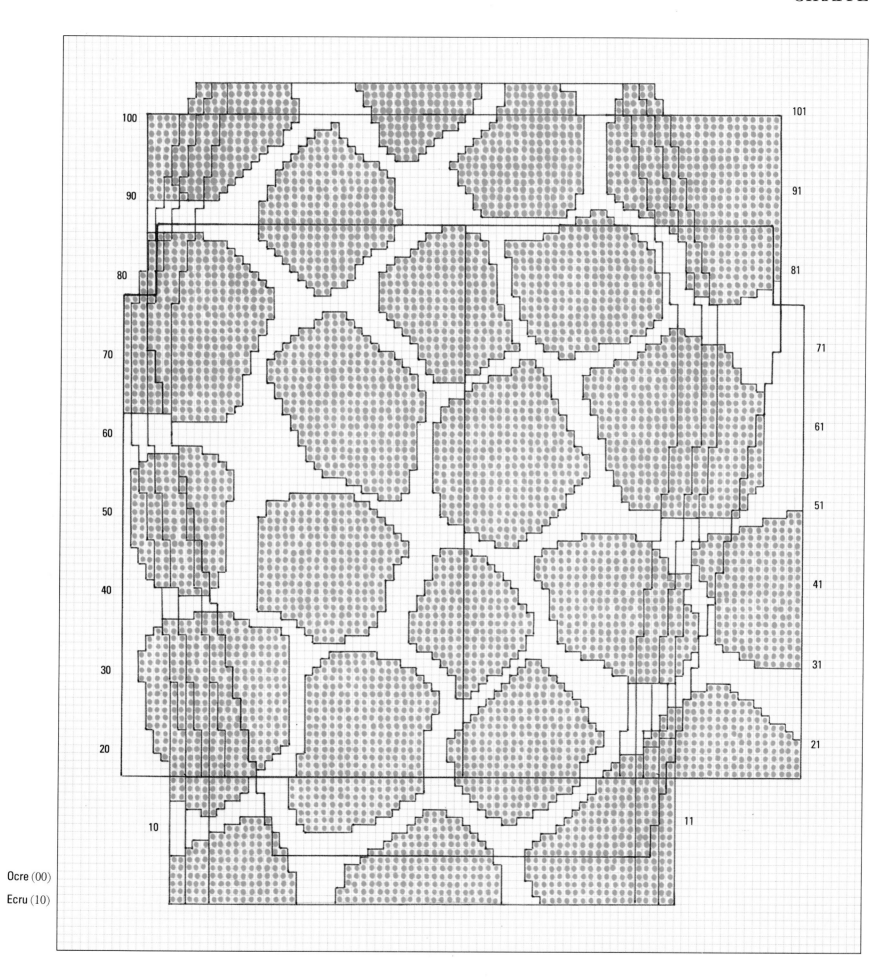

Ocre (00)
Ecru (10)

RIGHT FRONT

Using size 6 needles and ocre, cast on 43 sts.

Work 6 rows rib as given for back.

Next row: Rib 2, bind off 2 sts., rib to end.

Next row: Rib 39, turn, cast on 2 sts., turn, rib to end.

Work 7 more rows rib.

Inc. row: Rib 6, m.1, * rib 4, m.1; rep. from * to last 13 sts., rib 6 sts., turn and leave rem. 7 sts. on a stitch holder: 43 sts. Change to size 7 needles and work from center point of row 17 of chart, setting pat. as follows:

Row 17: K.1 ocre, k.4 ecru, k.16 ocre, k.5 ecru, k.11 ocre, k.6 ecru. Cont. working from chart shaping armhole by binding off 4 sts. at beg. of row 78: 39 sts.

Now work as given for left front from ** to ** until 29 rib rows have been completed, ending rib row 3.

Complete by working from *** to *** as given for left front.

SLEEVES

Using size 6 needles and ocre, cast on 37 sts.

Work 2½in in k.1, p.1 rib as given for back, ending rib row 1.

Inc. row: * Rib 3, m.1; rep. from * to last 4 sts., rib to end: 48 sts.

Change to size 7 needles and work from row 7 of chart, placing pat. as follows:

Row 7: K.16 ocre, k.4 ecru, k.16 ocre, k.10 ecru, k.2 ocre. Cont. working from chart, at the same time, shape sides by inc. 1 st. each end of 5th and every foll. 4th row until there are 80 sts. Work 29 rows even.

Bind off.

BUTTONBAND

Using size 6 needles and ocre, with RS of left front facing, join yarn to first st. on a stitch holder.

Work 100 rows in k.1, p.1 rib as given for back.

Leave sts. on a stitch stitch holder.

Stitch buttonband to left front using invisible seam.

BUTTONHOLE BAND

Using size 6 needles and ocre, with WS of right front facing, join yarn to first st. on stitch holder.

Starting rib row 2, work in k.1, p.1 rib as given for back until 24 rows have been worked from last buttonhole.

Next row: Rib 2, bind off 2 sts., rib to end.

Next row: Rib 3, turn, cast on 2 sts., turn, rib to end.

* Rib 24 rows, then work 2 buttonhole rows, rep. from * until 5 buttonholes have been worked.

Rib 4 rows, leave sts. on a stitch holder.

Join buttonhole band to right front using invisible seam.

NECKBAND

Join shoulder seams.

Using size 6 needles and ocre, with RS facing, k. across 7 sts. of buttonhole band, 7 sts. of right front, pick up and k.15 sts. up right front neck, 7 sts. at right back neck, 19 sts. at back neck, 7 sts. at left back neck, 15 sts. at left front neck, k. across 7 sts. of left front and 7 sts. of buttonband: 91 sts.

Bind off all sts.

COLLAR

Using size 6 needles and ocre, cast on 83 sts. Work 20 rows in k.1, p.1 rib as given for back. Bind off in rib. Starting at 5th st. on left front, with WS tog., join collar to neck, matching bound-off edges, stitch by stitch.

POCKETS (Knit 2)

Using size 7 needles and noir, cast on 20 sts.

Beg. with a k. row, work 23 rows st.st.

Row 24: Knit.

Row 25: Purl.

Row 26: K.2, k.2 tbl, k. to last 4 sts., k.2 tog., k.2.

Row 27: P.2, p.2 tog., p. to last 4 sts., p.2 tog. tbl, p.2.

Rep. rows 26 and 27 until 4 sts. rem.

Next row: K.2 tog. tbl, k.2 tog.

Next row: P.2 tog., break off yarn and pull through.

TO FINISH

Block and press pieces lightly under a damp cloth foll. yarn label instructions. Fold and press pocket flap to right side. Stitch point in place and sew on a small button. Position pockets by placing top edge just below ribbed yoke. Slipstitch or machine stitch in place. Backstitch or machine length of fringe across back just below ribbed yoke and around each armhole where ribbing begins and ends. Join side seams. Sew sleeve seams and cover seams with fringe from top of cuff to armhole. Pin sleeves in place, matching fringed sleeve seam to back yoke fringe. Sew in place. Sew on buttons.

Skirt

BACK AND FRONT

Longer length

Using size 6 needles and ecru, cast on 63 (69, 73) sts.

Work 5 rows in k.1, p.1 rib as given for jacket back.

Change to size 7 needles.

Dec. row: P.3 (1, 3), p.2 tog., * p.5 (6, 6), p.2 tog.; rep. from * to last 2 (2, 4) sts., p. to end: 54 (60, 64) sts.

Now work from row 1 of chart, placing pat. as follows:

Row 1: K.12 (15, 17) ocre, k.5 ecru, k.21 ocre, k.5 ecru, k.11 (14,16) ocre.

Cont. working from chart, at the same time inc. 1 st. each end of row 35 ** and every foll. 6th row until there are 64 (70, 74) sts.

Work 17 rows even.

Now dec.1 st. each end of next and every foll. 4th row until 50 (56, 60) sts. rem.

2nd and 3rd sizes only

P.1 row, then dec. 1 st. at each end of last row: 50 (54, 58) sts.

All sizes

Work 3 (1, 1) rows in pat., dec 1 st. at end of last row: 49 (53, 57) sts.

Change to size 6 needles and using ocre, work 2½in in k.1, p.1 rib as given for jacket back. **

Mini length

Using size 6 needles and ecru, cast on 59 (65, 69) sts.

Work 5 rows in k.1, p.1 rib as given for jacket back.

Change to size 7 needles.

Dec. row: P.5 (3, 1), p.2 tog., * p.4 (5, 6), p.2 tog.; rep. from * to last 4 (4, 2) sts., p. to end: 50 (56, 60) sts.

Now work from row 17 of chart, placing pat. as follows:

Row 17: K.2 (5, 7) ocre, k.3 ecru, k.16 ocre, k.4 ecru, k.16 ocre, k.5 ecru, k.4 (7, 9) ocre.

Cont. working from chart, at the same time, inc. 1 st. each end of row 25.

Now work as given for longer length from ** to **.

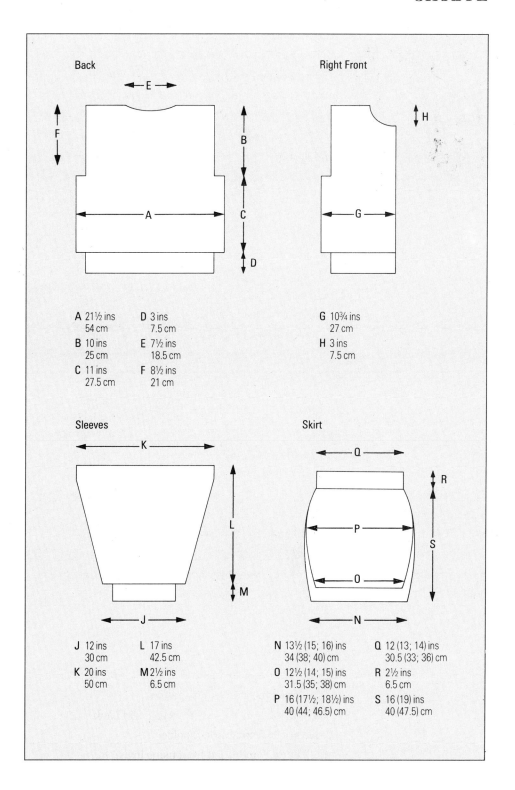

Back

A	21½ ins / 54 cm	D	3 ins / 7.5 cm
B	10 ins / 25 cm	E	7½ ins / 18.5 cm
C	11 ins / 27.5 cm	F	8½ ins / 21 cm

Right Front

G	10¾ ins / 27 cm
H	3 ins / 7.5 cm

Sleeves

J	12 ins / 30 cm	L	17 ins / 42.5 cm
K	20 ins / 50 cm	M	2½ ins / 6.5 cm

Skirt

N	13½ (15; 16) ins / 34 (38; 40) cm	Q	12 (13; 14) ins / 30.5 (33; 36) cm
O	12½ (14; 15) ins / 31.5 (35; 38) cm	R	2½ ins / 6.5 cm
P	16 (17½; 18½) ins / 40 (44; 46.5) cm	S	16 (19) ins / 40 (47.5) cm

TO FINISH

Block and press pieces lightly under a damp cloth foll. yarn label instructions. Join side seams leaving 6in on left side for zipper. Insert zipper. Sew fringe along side seams, from top of hem to base of waistband.

There are three species of Zebra, all of them found in Africa. The most familiar is the stocky Plains or Common Zebra which is still abundant on the grasslands and savannahs of East Africa. Less well known and rarer are the Mountain Zebra of south-west Africa and the elegant Grevy's Zebra of southern Somalia and Ethiopia and northern Kenya. Mountain Zebras have been intensively persecuted by farmers who thought that they competed with domestic livestock for grazing and water. Numbers were reduced from over 70,000 in the 1950s to around 7,000 by the end of the 1970s. Fortunately, the remaining Mountain Zebras are relatively well protected in several different national parks and reserves. Much less secure is Grevy's Zebra, which has suffered badly from hunting and from prolonged droughts. Few Grevy's Zebras are protected in reserves and their numbers are still decreasing.

Burchells ZEBRA

▶ The "Modernist" arrangement of the Zebra stripes lends itself so readily to textile design. This easy-to-make outfit in cotton uses the stripes on the skirt and the yoke of the sweater. The fringing represents the Zebra's thick black mane.

SIZES
Sweater: to fit 32 (34/36, 38)in bust.
Skirt: 33 (35, 37)in hips.

MATERIALS
Pingouin Corrida 4 (medium-weight cotton)
Sweater
11 × 1¾oz balls Blanc (shade 501)
2 × 1¾oz balls Noir (shade 528)
2¼yd of black fringe
4 × ⅝in white buttons
Skirt
5 × 1¾oz balls Blanc (shade 501)
2 × 1¾oz balls Noir (shade 528)
6in white zipper
A pair each of sizes 3 and 6 knitting needles
Stitch holder

GAUGE
20 sts. and 26 rows to 4in over pat. worked on size 6 needles

To save time, take time to check gauge.

NOTES
Directions for larger sizes are given in parentheses (). When working pattern, use separate, small balls of yarn for each black and white area. This will avoid looping or weaving the yarn and will keep the gauge more even. When joining in a new color, leave an end of about 2in for weaving in later. When changing color, twist yarns together at back of work to avoid making a hole.

Sweater
BACK
** Using size 3 needles and blanc, cast on 93 (97, 101) sts.
Rib row 1: K.1, * p.1, k.1; rep from * to end.
Rib row 2: P.1 , * k.1, p.1; rep. from * to end.
Rep. these 2 rows once, inc. 1 st. at end of last row: 94 (98, 102) sts.
Change to size 6 needles and work 34 (36, 38) rows st.st.

*"Burchell's Zebra"
modeled by Caron Keating,
co-presenter of Blue Peter,
the popular BBC children"s
program. Swimming with
sharks in the Pacific Ocean
and with wild dolphins off
the coast of Ireland have
been two of Caron"s
amazing assignments for
Blue Peter.*

Noir (528)

Blanc (501)

Shape armholes

Bind off 4 sts.at beg. of next 2 rows: 86 (90, 94) sts.

Work 4 (8, 8) rows even, then 2 rows noir.

Now work from row 51 of chart **.

Joining in small balls of color, set pat. as follows:

Row 51: K.6 (8, 10) blanc, k.4 noir, 3 blanc, 6 noir, 2 blanc, 4 noir, 5 blanc, 4 noir, 4 blanc, 5 noir, 7 blanc, 5 noir, 2 blanc, 1 noir, 7 blanc, 2 noir, 17 blanc, 1 noir, 1 (3, 5) blanc.

Cont. until row 100 has been completed.

Shape back neck

Next row: Working in pat., k.33 (35, 37) sts., turn and leave rem. sts. on a stitch holder.

Work on these sts. only.

Next row: Bind off 4 sts., p. to end.

K.1 row.

Next row: Bind off 3 (4, 4) sts., p. to end.

Bind off.

Return to rem. sts.

With RS facing, slip first 20 sts. onto a stitch holder.

Rejoin yarn and k. to end.

Now complete to match first side, reversing all shaping.

FRONT

Work as given for back from ** to **.

Divide for front opening

Joining in small balls of color, work left half of chart from row 51, setting pat. as follows:

Row 51: K.6 (8, 10) blanc, 4 noir, 3 blanc, 6 noir, 2 blanc, 4 noir, 5 blanc, 4 noir, 4 blanc, 2 noir, turn and leave rem. sts. on a stitch holder: 40 (42, 44) sts.

Work in pat. on these sts. only for left front until row 92 has been completed.

Shape left front neck

Next row: K.33 (35, 37) sts., turn and leave rem. 7 sts. on a stitch holder.

Dec. 1 st. at neck edge only until 26 (27, 29) sts. rem.

Work 4 (3, 3) rows even.

Bind off.

Return to sts. for right front.

With RS facing and using blanc, rejoin yarn and bind off first 6 sts. Foll. right half of chart from row 51, work in pat.

to end: 40 (42, 44) sts. Cont. in pat. from chart until row 93 has been completed.

Shape right front neck

Next row: P.33 (35, 37) sts., turn and leave rem. 7 sts. on a stitch stitch holder.

Now complete to match left front, reversing all shaping.

SLEEVES

Using size 3 needles and blanc, cast on 47 (51, 51) sts.

Work 17 rows in rib as given for back.

Inc. row: (WS) Rib 3 (5, 5), m.1, * rib 5, m.1; rep. from * to last 4 (6, 6) sts., rib to end: 56 (60, 60) sts.

Change to size 6 needles and work in st.st., inc. 1 st. at each end of 5th and every foll. 4th row until there are 96 (100, 100) sts.

Cont. even until sleeve measures 18½ (20, 20¼)in from beg. of sleeve.

Bind off.

BUTTONBAND

Using size 3 needles and blanc, with RS facing, pick up and k.29 sts. along left front.

P.1 row.

Work 8 rows in rib as given for back.

Bind off in rib.

BUTTONHOLE BAND

Using size 3 needles and blanc, with RS facing, pick up and k.29 sts. along right front.

P.1 row

Work 4 rows in rib as given for back.

Next row: Rib 7, yo, k.2 tog., * rib 6, yo, k.2 tog.; rep from * to last 4 sts., rib to end.

Work 3 more rows in rib.

Bind off in rib.

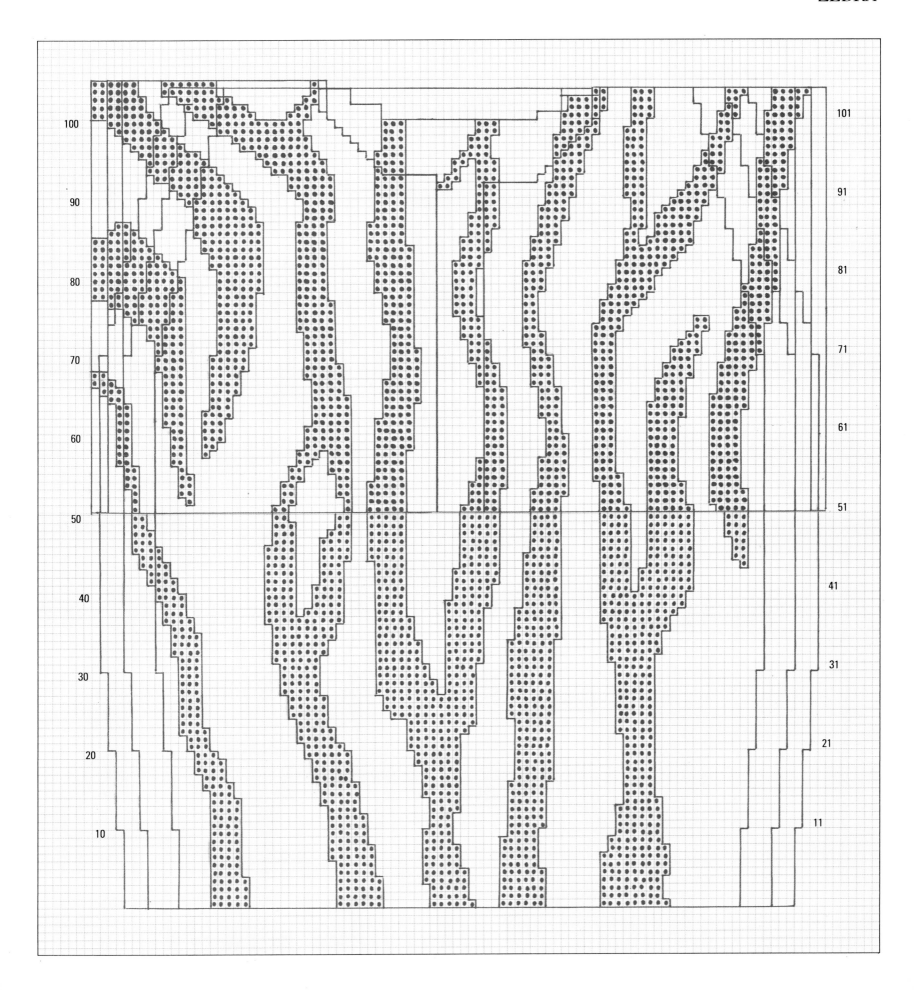

ZEBRA

NECKBAND

Join both shoulder seams.

Using size 3 needles and blanc, with RS facing, pick up and k.8 sts. across buttonhole band, k.7 sts. from stitch holder, pick up and k.12 (13, 13) sts. up right front neck, 10 (11, 11) sts. down right back neck, k.20 sts. from stitch holder, pick up and k.10 (11, 11) sts. up left back neck, 13 (14, 14) sts. down left front neck, k. 7 sts. from stitch holder, pick up and k.8 sts. across buttonband: 95 (99, 99) sts.

P.1 row.

Bind off.

COLLAR

Using size 3 needles and blanc, cast on 95 (99, 99) sts.

Work 22 rows in rib as given for back.

Next row: Rib 3, yo, k.2 tog., rib to end.

Work 3 rows rib.

Bind off in rib.

TO FINISH

Block and press pieces lightly under a damp cloth foll. yarn label instructions. Stitch buttonhole band and buttonband to bound-off sts. at center front.

Machine or backstitch fringe across front and back yokes, stitching across 2 rows noir, and around armhole edge of yokes.

Stitch bound-off edge of collar to neckband. Joining bound-off edge of armhole to underarms, sew in sleeves, then join side and sleeve seams, sew on buttons.

Skirt (Back and front alike)

Using size 3 needles and blanc, cast on 83 (91, 97) sts.

Work 6 rows rib as given for sweater back.

Change to size 6 needles.

Dec. row: P.5 (5, 7), p.2 tog., * p.5 (6, 6), p.2 tog.; rep. from * to last 6 (4, 8) sts., p. to end: 72 (80, 86) sts.

Work rows 1–104 from chart, shaping sides as shown: 60 (68, 74) sts.

Next row: Using blanc, k.2 tog., k. to end: 59 (67, 73) sts.

Change to size 3 needles and starting with rib row 2 as given for sweater back, work 2in in k.1, p.1 rib.

Bind off in rib.

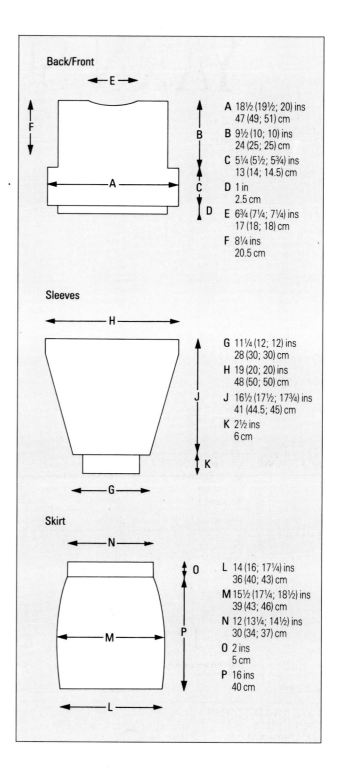

Back/Front

A 18½ (19½; 20) ins
47 (49; 51) cm
B 9½ (10; 10) ins
24 (25; 25) cm
C 5¼ (5½; 5¾) ins
13 (14; 14.5) cm
D 1 in
2.5 cm
E 6¾ (7¼; 7¼) ins
17 (18; 18) cm
F 8¼ ins
20.5 cm

Sleeves

G 11¼ (12; 12) ins
28 (30; 30) cm
H 19 (20; 20) ins
48 (50; 50) cm
J 16½ (17½; 17¾) ins
41 (44.5; 45) cm
K 2½ ins
6 cm

Skirt

L 14 (16; 17¼) ins
36 (40; 43) cm
M 15½ (17¼; 18½) ins
39 (43; 46) cm
N 12 (13¼; 14½) ins
30 (34; 37) cm
O 2 ins
5 cm
P 16 ins
40 cm

TO FINISH

Block and press pieces lightly under a damp cloth foll. yarn label instructions. Join side seams leaving an opening of 6in on left side seam. Sew in zipper using machine or backstitch.

YARN SUPPLIERS

	PATONS	EMU	PINGOUIN	HAYFIELD	SCHEEPJESWOOL
US	Patons Yarns 212 Middlesex Avenue Chester CT 06412	c/o Plymouth Yarn PO Box 28 500 Lafayette St. PA 19007	Pingouin Laninter Corp. PO Box 1542 Mt. Pleasant SC 29465	c/o Cascade Yarns 204 3rd Avenue S. Seattle WA 98104	c/o Juniper Yarn and Craft Co Inc. 199 Trade Zone Drive Rononkona NY 11779
UK	Patons & Baldwins Ltd Alloa Clackmannanshire EK10 TEG Scotland Beehive softblend DK	Emu International Ltd Leeds Road Idle Bradford West Yorkshire BD10 9TE	Pingouin French Wools Ltd Station House 81–83 Fulham High St. London SW6 3JW	Hayfield Hayfield Textiles Ltd Glusburn Keighley West Yorkshire BD20 8QP	
CANADA	Patons & Baldwins Ltd 1001 Rost Lawn Avenue Toronto ON M6B 1B8 Beehive DK	S. R. Kertzer Ltd 105A Winges Road Woodbridge Ontario L4L 6C2	1500 Rue Jules Poitras Ville St. Laurent, Quebec	Mr K. Ehman Craftsmen Distributors Inc 4166 Halifax Street Burnaby British Columbia V5C 3XC	
AUSTRALIA	Coats & Patons Pty Ltd 89–91 Peters Avenue Mulgrave Victoria 3170 Beehive 8-ply	Karingal Vic/Tas Pty Ltd 6 Macro Court Rowville Victoria 3178	47–57 Collins St Alexandria New South Wales 2015 or PO Box 163 Beaconsfield New South Wales 2014	Karingal (Emu supplier) Vic Tas Pty Ltd 359 Dorset Road Bayswater Victoria 3153	
NEW ZEALAND	Coats & Patons (NZ) Ltd 263 Ti Rakau Drive Pakuranga Auckland N2 Beehive 8-ply	Enzed Sewing Ltd 40 Sir William Avenue East Tamaki Auckland PO Box 61–087	Not available (see substitution chart or contact Australian supplier)	Not available (for details see Australia)	
SOUTH AFRICA	Not available (see substitution chart)	Brasen Hobby PO Box 6405 Johannesburg 2000	Pingouin Yarns Saprotex (Pty) Ltd PO Box 306, New Germany 3620	Brasch Hobby (Emu supplier) 57 La Rochelle Road Trojan Johannesburg 2197	

YARN SUBSTITUTION

If you are unable to obtain the recommended yarns, use this simple substitution guide or ask your yarn shop for assistance.

GARMENTS	YARN SUBSTITUTES	GARMENTS	YARN SUBSTITUTES
BADGER/WILD FLOWERS GIANT PANDAS BREACHING WHALES BLACK RHINO	Any thick, bulky yarns: e.g., *Emu* Snowball; *Patons* Parade; *Hayfield* Grampian Chunky; *Emu* Supermatch Chunky with *Emu* Supermatch DK.	GT. BARRIER REEF ZEBRA SWANS/DAFFODILS	Any medium-weight cotton: e.g. *Pingouin* Cotonade, Coton Mercerise no. 4; *Patons* Cotton Perle, Cotton Soft or Baby Cotton; *Schachenmayr* Alpha; *Scheepjeswool* Mayflower DK.
POLAR BEARS GIRAFFE	Any Aran, or softer bulky yarns: e.g. *Hayfield* Grampian Aran, or Brig Aran; *Patons* Diploma Aran; *Emu* Supermatch Chunky.	MOUNTAIN GORILLA	Any medium-weight mohair yarns: e.g., *Emu* Filigree; *Patons* Mohair Visions; *Pingouin* Mohair or Pidou. Any bulky yarns: e.g. *Emu* Supermatch Chunky; *Patons* Parade.
INDIAN/WHITE TIGERS LIONESSES GOLDEN EAGLE BABY SEAL AFRICAN ELEPHANT	Any knitting-worsted weight wool yarns: e.g., *Pingouin* 4 Pingouins, Confort, France +, Challenge 4, Pure Laine no. 4; *Patons* Beehive or Diploma; *Hayfield* Grampian DK; *Emu* Supermatch DK; *Schachenmayr* Extra		Please remember to *check your gauge*, when substituting yarns, and adjust needle size accordingly.

KNITTING KNOW-HOW

Duplicate Stitch

Thread the needle with the required colored yarn and fasten to the back of the work.
Bring the needle through to the right side of the fabric through the center of the lower point of the stitch. Insert the needle at the top right-hand side of the same stitch. Hold the needle in a horizontal position and pull it through the top left-hand side of the stitch. Now insert again into the base of the stitch to the left of where the needle came out at the start of the stitch. Keep the yarn loose enough to lie on top of the work and cover the knitted stitch.

ABBREVIATIONS

alt.	alternate (every other)
beg.	begin(ning)
CC	contrasting color
cont.	continu(e)(ing)
dec.	decreas(e)(ing)
foll.	follow(s)(ing)
inc.	increas(e)(ing)
in	inch(es)
k.	knit
m.1	make one stitch*
MC	main color
oz	ounce(s)
p.	purl
pat.	pattern
psso	pass slip stitch over
rem.	remain(s)(ing)
rep.	repeat(s)(ing)
RS	right side
sl.	slip
st(s).	stitch(es)
st.st.	stockinette stitch
tbl	through back of loop
tog.	together
WS	wrong side
yo	yarn over (needle)

* Insert left needle from front to back under horizontal strand between last st. worked and next st. on left needle to make a new st., then knit tbl of this new st. – called make one stitch.

READING CHARTS

The patterns in this book all use charts. Each chart consists of a grid, sometimes with the actual shape being knitted marked up in the squares. Each square represents one stitch and each horizontal line of squares represents one row.

Unless otherwise stated in the directions the design shown on the chart is worked in stockinette stitch – all odd-numbered chart rows being read from right to left and worked as knit stitches (right-side rows) and all even-numbered chart rows being read from left to right and worked as purl stitches (wrong-side rows).

Each square shows which color yarn is to be used for that stitch.

If on the design you are working there is only a small motif to be worked, then the chart is only given for that area of the sweater and the directions will tell you where to place the motif within the row. All stitches outside the chart are then worked in the main color.

If the chart is for the full section of the piece you are knitting, then it will usually indicate any shaping that needs to be done. If the number of squares changes at the side, armhole and neck edges, then increase or decrease that number of stitches at that point on the row you are working.

At the center front neck, where there are usually quite a few stitches to be shaped, either leave the center stitches on a stitch holder or refer to the pattern instructions to see if it tells you to bind them off.

CHANGING COLORS

When working from the charts it is necessary to use several different colors, very often within the same row.

If there are very small areas to be worked in any of the colors, then wind a small amount of yarn either into a small ball or onto a bobbin. This will make working with a lot of colors easier and help to stop them getting tangled.

When joining in a new color at the beginning of a row, insert the knitting needle into the first stitch, make a loop in the new yarn, leaving an end to be later woven in, then place this loop over the needle and complete the stitch.

When joining in a new color in the middle of a row, work in the first color to the point where the new color is needed, then insert the needle into the next stitch and complete with the new color in the same way as for joining in at the beginning of a row.

When changing color along a row always make sure that the color that is being used is twisted around the next color to be used, otherwise the two stitches willl not be linked together and a hole will form between them.

Changing Color

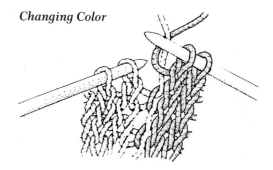

BLOCKING AND PRESSING

After knitting all the pieces for the garment, first weave in all the ends securely, then for a better finished look block all the pieces.

Firstly cover a large area with a thick blanket and a piece of clean fabric such as a sheet.

Lay out each piece of the garment and pin out to the correct shape.

If the yarn can be pressed, then cover with a damp cloth and press each piece lightly avoiding all ribbing. Do not move the iron over the fabric, but keep picking it up and placing it lightly down again.

If the yarn cannot be pressed, then cover with a damp cloth and leave until completely dry.

EMBROIDERY

Some of the designs have added embroidery to give extra detail. The first of these is called Backstitch and this is used whenever a line is needed. The second stitch used is a French Knot and this is used whenever spots or dots are needed.

Backstitch

Thread the needle with the required colored yarn and fasten to the back of the work.
Bring the needle through to the right side of the fabric.

Backstitch

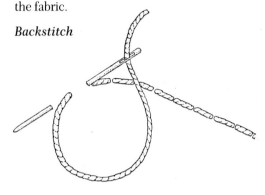

Insert the needle back through the fabric about ³⁄₁₆in to the right of where the yarn was brought through and then bring it back out again about ³⁄₁₆in to the left of the first stitch. Bring the needle through, pulling the yarn gently. Now insert the needle back into the fabric at the end of the first stitch and bring it out again ³⁄₁₆in farther along. Continue in this way until the line has been completed, then fasten off securely.

French Knot and Half French Knot

Thread the needle with the required colored yarn and fasten to the back of the work.
Bring the needle through to the right side of the fabric at the position for the knot. Take a

French Knot

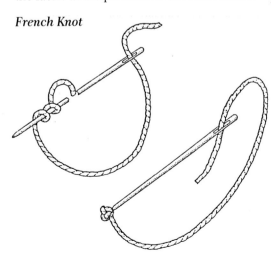

small stitch of the fabric and wind the yarn twice around the point of the needle for a french knot and once for a half french knot.
Pull the needle carefully through the fabric at the base of the knot and fasten off on the wrong side.

FINISHING

Once the pieces have been blocked refer to the finishing instructions for the order in which to assemble them. When joining seams where the pattern needs to match at any point then the invisible seam method gives a more professional finish, but a backstitched seam is slightly easier and with care can give just as neat a finish.

Invisible seam

Lay both pieces of fabric to be joined on a flat surface with the right side facing. Thread the needle with matching yarn and join it to the lower edge of one of the pieces.
Take the needle and insert it into the center of the first stitch at the lower edge of the second piece of knitting.

Invisible Seam

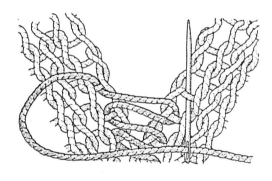

Bring the needle back up through the stitch above, so picking up the bar between the rows of stitches. Pull the yarn through, then take the needle back across to the first piece of knitting and repeat. Pull the yarn gently so that the two pieces of knitting are drawn together. Insert the needle back into the second piece of knitting, in the same place as the needle came out, and pick up the next bar above, then repeat again on the first piece of knitting. Continue in this way to the top of the seam, gently pulling the yarn every few stitches to close the seam.
After the last stitch fasten off securely.

Backstitch seam

Place the two pieces to be joined right sides together.

Backstitch Seam

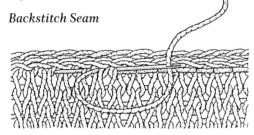

and fasten to the beginning of the seam with a couple of stitches.
Insert the needle through both thicknesses and bring it back out again about ³⁄₁₆in along the seam. Bring the needle through, pulling the yarn gently. Insert the needle back into the same place as it was inserted the first time but this time bring it out about ³⁄₁₆in farther along from the last stitch. Pull the yarn through.
Now insert the needle back into the fabric at the end of the first stitch and bring it out again ³⁄₁₆in farther along. Continue in this way to the end of the seam, then fasten off securely.

AFTERCARE

After all the hard work of knitting and finishing your garment it is important to wash it correctly in order to keep it looking new.
Always keep a yarn label from one of the balls of yarn that the garment was knitted with, so that you can always refer to the washing instructions for that yarn. If there are no washing instructions on the yarn label, or if you have not kept one, then hand wash only in cool water. Either squeeze gently or give a short spin, then lay the garment flat and ease into shape. Dry flat, away from heat or direct sunlight.

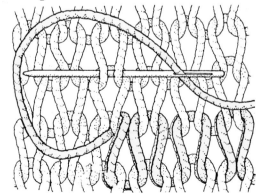

ACKNOWLEDGEMENTS

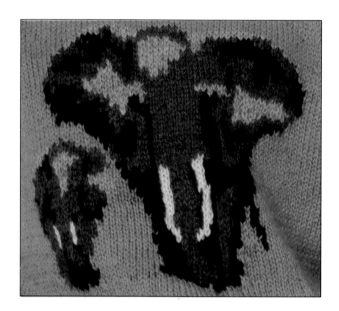

Ruth and Karen would like to thank everyone involved in the book, especially our wonderful models.

Kim Knott and his studio assistant, Nick Pearson.

Jane Cohen, Celia Hunter, Mary Vango, Lino of Gelrard and Lino, Charlie Green and special thanks to Keith at Smile for Marie Helvin's hair.

Winifred Muir, Christine Kingdom, Margaret Slater, Debbie Hudson, Sandra Cook, and Rose for their enthusiasm and efficiency in supplying yarn.

Our knitters: Dorothy Herring, Sue Williams, Olwyn Webb, Auntie Dorothy, June, and Margaret.